# Parenting
## with BALLS

*For us.*

# Parenting
## with BALLS

NEW HOLLAND

## Ian Newbold

First published in 2013 by New Holland Publishers Pty Ltd
London • Sydney • Cape Town • Auckland

Garfield House 86–88 Edgware Road London W2 2EA United Kingdom
1/66 Gibbes Street Chatswood NSW 2067 Australia
Wembley Square First Floor Solan Road Gardens Cape Town 8001 South Africa
218 Lake Road Northcote Auckland New Zealand

www.newhollandpublishers.com

ISBN 9781742572888

Managing Director: Fiona Schultz
Publisher: Alan Whiticker
Project Editor: Kate Sherington
Designer: Kimberley Pearce
Proofreader: Victoria Fisher
Production Director: Olga Dementiev
Printer: Toppan Leefung Printing Ltd (China)

10 9 8 7 6 5 4 3 2 1

Keep up with New Holland Publishers on Facebook
www.facebook.com/NewHollandPublishers

# Contents

# 1.
# The mother of all bad wake-up calls

As a relatively new parent, 2am was not an unusual time to be woken from a perfect sleep. My seven-month-old son was regularly making a fuss at that time of the night, or morning – lines like that tend to get blurred upon becoming a parent, much as your vision is being woken at that time of day. My child would switch to an escalating cry mode because he wanted a feed, because he needed changing, because he'd lost his dummy, or simply because he was awake and wanted everyone in the house to know it. This time was different. This time it was my wife waking me up. And it was not to point out that I was sleeping through one of my 'turns' tending to our nocturnally squawking baby.

No, not this time. My son, Max, was sound asleep in his travel cot beside our bed. This in itself was pleasing, as we weren't sure how well it would go down with him before we set off on our quaint cottage holiday to Somerset. Something else was bothering his wonderful mother, Samantha, who was always 'Sam' unless I really wanted to grab her attention.

'I don't feel right,' Sam said.

'Well, you've never been right, beautiful. You're going to have to be more specific,' I replied.

It really was unusual for Sam to get me up, and as she'd not gone to bed troubled or stressed – quite the opposite in fact – I was perplexed as to what the problem could be.

'I've got chest pains, and I'm really, really burning up,' she said.

'Shit,' I thought. She didn't look good. She looked exactly as she'd said – in some pain, flushed and perspiring profusely. Being 150 miles from home also made the situation a little unnerving, but we were both remaining calm. These things happen, it will probably be nothing, she's had a reaction to something, she'll be fine.

However, I decided it was unusual enough, and not worth taking any risks, to make an emergency call for an ambulance or doctor. Sam agreed. We were still very jovial and not overly concerned about her immediate health or what this problem could be. It just warranted proper attention.

We were parents now and not only obligated to take care of ourselves for ourselves, but more importantly, for our child.

We were holidaying with Samantha's parents, so I went and gently woke them. I tried not to panic them, just hoping to make them aware of what was going on and put them on standby for childcare. Sam's mother joined us in our bedroom while I made the call to emergency services.

Despite being in the middle of nowhere I had a decent telephone signal. The telephone operator went through all the formalities, deciding very quickly to deploy a paramedic by car, with an ambulance placed on standby. I think the minute you mention chest pains they have someone dispatched and on their way to you – not that I'm giving you a top tip of how to get urgent medical attention. But the operator was struggling to find our location on her GPS system, so these vehicles were headed only to our vicinity, not necessarily directly for us. Sam's dad went outside to flag down those people and vehicles dispatched and looking for us.

Samantha's breathing had become more laboured while I'd been making this phone call. By now I was relaying her answers to the medical questions the emergency telephone operator was asking. There was very little communication between Sam and I. Instead, I was merely acting as her mouthpiece to communicate to the emergency services. Whether I was blinding myself to the situation, remaining calm with the words 'She's going to be fine in a minute' repeating in my head, I still didn't feel like this was going to be anything more than something we joked about in the future. 'Remember the time I woke your parents up in the middle of the night on their first holiday with their grandson?' It wouldn't have been the worst faux pas I'd made in front of the in-laws. It probably wouldn't even make the top twenty. But I was sure we'd be laughing about what could have been a serious situation some time in the near future.

I was wrong. This was a grave situation, the gravest I had ever, probably will ever be, presented with.

Samantha made an indescribable, horrific gargling noise, her eyes rolled into the back of her head, and she lost consciousness.

'You're going to have to perform CPR, Mr Newbold,' the voice on the phone said, like she had eyes in the room. With the phone jammed between my shoulder and ear, I did exactly that, aided by Samantha's mother. Even as I acted without hesitation, the situation seemed so ridiculous and very surreal. How had we got to this point? I remembered the CPR training I'd done a year or so ago, on a dummy that tasted of ageing plastic and alcohol wipes, but this was my wife. My son's beautiful mother. Caressing her lips had always been a delightful and delicate experience. Now it was merely so I could get my oxygen into her lungs and bloodstream.

'Where the hell is the ambulance?' I would scream, while I was making compressions or while Samantha's mother was taking her turn blowing air into her daughter.

'Not far away,' was the constant reply on the phone. And after a period that felt like an eternity, but could have been as little as a few minutes, the professionals did arrive. They were shepherded in by Samantha's dad. Upon news of their arrival, the operator hung up, and we awaited the intervention of the experts. They seemed to be somewhat shocked by the seriousness of the situation now presented to them. I guess – like me only moments before – they thought they were going to be dealing with a chest complaint. Now they were dealing with a young mother fighting for her life. It took them a few seconds to take that in, but then they leapt into action.

Max's travel cot was removed from beside our bed. Such was my focus on Samantha that I hadn't concerned myself with where he was. I guessed that one of his grandparents had put him into the other bedroom. Samantha was moved to the floor where the travel cot had been, in readiness for the CPR to continue. The two paramedics took over, saying, 'Sam, can you hear me? Sam, Sam?'

Because I'd been making the emergency call, focusing all my attention on that, I hadn't been talking to Samantha. I couldn't recall encouraging her to wake up, to fight or to hear me. I don't know what difference, if any at all, it would have made, but I was aware of having done no more than I was told at the point the paramedics tried to rouse her.

The surreal nature of the situation was taking over and in danger of consuming me. It was like I wasn't really there. Who was this person, laid out prostrate on the floor? Why were these neon-jacketed people in our bedroom? Was I still asleep?

Snapping me out of my daze, the two paramedics sent me out to their ambulance to fetch a medical bag, described to me a cube with a green cross on it. I ran out of our picturesque cottage as fast as I could into the absolute darkness outside. Being in the English countryside at night is eerie at the best of times, but I couldn't see or hear a thing other than the scramble of the gravel under my feet. The grey shale probably only slowed me down by a few seconds, but it felt like I was trying to sprint on a sand dune, as well as being deafened by it. I needed to be back with this bag in an instant, not thwarted by this loose surface hell.

Jumping into the back of the ambulance, I desperately searched for the bag the paramedics wanted. I couldn't find it and I was soon getting desperate. Was this going to be my wife's downfall? A stray green bag? My inability to find anything in a rush?

I ran back over the gravel empty-handed, straight into our bedroom, and literally knocked the paramedic straddling my wife off her, screaming, 'I'll do this, you get the bag, go, go.' The stunned medic disappeared, only to reappear in a flash with the bag. I knew what I was doing, or could certainly be directed by the remaining medic. And hadn't been able to find this bag. While we continued with CPR, the bag's adrenaline was administered in an extra effort to kick-start Sam's struggling heart, and at this point we got our ray of hope.

'We have a heartbeat,' the paramedic said.

Reluctantly, and exhausted, I gave way to the returning green-bag-bearing second medic, then shared the news of hope with Samantha's very distressed parents. I can't speak for them, but I think we all shared a feeling that everything was going to be okay, that this was not when and how my wife's life was going to end. Certainly we let our hope win out against our fear of the opposite at that point. This was Sam. The one upon whom we were all most reliant. She had to be okay. She would be okay.

And then.

'Samanatha's heart has stopped again. We need to get her to the hospital.'

These words, and the reality that we had been kidding ourselves only moments before, hit us very hard.

I was dazed. Hoping I'd wake up soon.

Shocked.

Confused.

My own adrenaline, the powerful juice that had allowed me to confidently control the situation and remain focused, without unnecessary drama or panic, was dwindling, as I suddenly understood the reality of what was happening.

I was witnessing the death of my wife.

I took the journey to the hospital in the back of the ambulance with Samantha, once again assisting the paramedic as the other one drove. It was clear they, and I, were doing everything possible to preserve her life, but I'd already started to accept that our efforts would be in vain.

'She's gone, hasn't she?' I asked, without really expecting an answer.

I'd never seen a dead person up close, but I recalled that my CPR trainer had said that sometimes you just can't resuscitate people. You simply *know* when someone has died. It was these words that I found more convincing than the medic's, who said, 'Let's see what they can do at the hospital.'

Emergency staff at the hospital were fully prepared when we arrived. They had clearly been well briefed on the sad situation about to land on them. There were people everywhere. Someone jumped on top of Samantha and CPR continued as she was wheeled on a trolley into the hospital.

This time I wasn't going to be a member of the team trying to save her life. My part was done. I was deposited in a waiting room and told to stay put. I could stand being on my own in that room for about 30 seconds. Instead I chose to pace the corridor, waiting to be interrupted by either the arrival of Sam's parents, or a doctor with news.

Sam's folks, and our son, arrived first. In fact, I think the hospital staff were waiting for them. We were called around to the theatre where Sam was being worked on. The scene there was very different to that in the bedroom of our holiday cottage. There were lots of people, lots of equipment, lots of machines, but ultimately they were all working to the same unsuccessful end – to breathe life back into Samantha.

I'm not sure the doctor ever actually said the words, 'Your wife has died, Mr Newbold.' But I knew that's what he was saying. He succinctly summarised the night's events: how we'd tried to resuscitate Sam, that she'd briefly regained a faint heartbeat, but that there had been no other signs of life for a sustained period. It was time to stop working on her.

The pain was overwhelming. But there was nothing that anyone else or I could do to change the fact that Sam had gone. Her laid-out body had clearly become only the vessel in which she'd lived her life; now it was empty, and she was no longer in it. I accepted what I was being told and Samantha was officially pronounced dead.

My wife had died, my son's mother had died, my in-laws' child, their princess, had died. And a big part of me died, too.

For the last couple of hours I'd pretty much ignored my son. He was mainly sleeping, in no immediate danger, and there were others able to tend to him if he needed anything. But now he needed me. He needed me more than ever. At least, that's what I convinced myself. In reality, it was me that needed him.

'Where is my boy?' I asked tearily. He was sleeping in his car seat, propped up on a hospital bed. He was peaceful, unaware of the horrendous loss he'd just suffered.

We were alone.

There was no more I could do for Samantha. But there was everything I needed to do for my boy.

# 2.
# Goodnight and
# God bless

Samantha was born with a heart defect called aortic stenosis. This meant that one of her main heart valves was narrowed and that her heart, the muscle that pumps blood around the body, was working harder on one side than on the other. It is a relatively common disorder, one that needed intervention as a 9-year-old child, and to be checked annually thereafter, but not one that hindered Sam's day-to-day life. When we were planning a family, I think even before we'd planned the wedding, I'd accompany Sam on her annual ECGs and consultations, partly just as support – trying to make hospital visits a little more interesting for her – but also to consult the experts about our plans, seeking their latest advice and acting on it if necessary.

Consultants always seemed surprised by our questions. 'No one has told you that you can't have children, have they?' they'd reply. Which, of course, they hadn't, but we always wanted to check if there was anything we could do to make a pregnancy easier on Sam's dickie ticker (how she loved that reference).

'Just, like anyone, be in the best shape you can, eat well and exercise, and let us know when the magic happens,' they said. Okay, they probably didn't say the last bit, but it was very much general advice. We appreciated that we'd probably need to see the cardiologist throughout her pregnancy, but never were we advised that having kids was a bad idea for Sam. It was always nice to meet other patients in waiting rooms with the same heart condition, who'd had families. Their experiences gave us real-life evidence of what the experts were telling us.

So, armed with all that information, we went ahead with out plans. We got pregnant.

We weren't lucky the first time, and Samantha miscarried.

It was horrific. I'd been around people who'd suffered the same loss, but had never really understood how it might feel. Honestly, to my shame now, I had some idea that miscarriage might be a natural medical clear out of some kind, a necessity to allow eventual safe passage of a healthy baby. And whilst appreciating it wasn't a nice thing to go through, I quietly thought that it was in no way comparable to the loss of a living soul. That's the point I'd missed. Miscarried babies are living souls, ones that, for whatever reason, were never meant to 'make it'. And no matter how many 'probably for the bests' you hear, it doesn't make it any easier to deal with. It was something we faced together, bringing us even closer, and sharpening our parenting potential.

With all that in mind, when Sam got pregnant with Max it wasn't a joyous and relaxed experience. We were both delighted, for sure, but inside we knew we were a long way from a healthy birth. I saw it as my job to keep Samantha calm and well, and a big part of that was appearing calm myself, and taking on whatever I needed to, in order to reduce any potential strain, both physical and psychological, on her.

Sam was known not to appreciate bad service, rudeness or – her number one pet hate – queue jumpers. When encountering such things, she would often erupt, my mini-yet-ferocious volcano. Sam's maiden name was Bagnall, so these volcanic eruptions were known as 'Bagnall moments'. The tail end of a Bagnall moment would often be directed my way, as I had failed to intervene. My laidback – and sometimes shy and lazy – nature meant that I would often fail to be bothered to the same extent that Sam was about some grievance, and did little more than put me in a bad mood.

But for Samantha's pregnancy, my attitude changed. I needed to step up. If these things were going to upset my wife, then they were going to affect me too, or I was certainly going to pretend they did. I felt that these 'Bagnall moments', or the very opportunity for them to occur, needed to be limited, eradicated even, during her pregnancy. So for that, and many other reasons, I was on hand for all the scans, meetings with the cardiologists, obstetricians and other professionals. It wasn't that the meetings themselves would be overly stressful, but simple things like finding a place to park, having the right change, getting directions to where we needed to be, and meeting grumpy and unhelpful staff at pretty much all those points, needed to be handled by me.

I was, in short, a hands-on expectant father. I immersed myself in information, making sure I knew at least as much as my wife did, enough to question the healthcare professionals, and for my knowledge to be good enough that I could – at the very least – get them to take me seriously.

Because of Samantha's pre-existing heart condition, the birth, and her birth plan, were pretty much dictated to us by collective medical expertise. I think it was our final say, but we'd have struggled to get through the pre-requisites of an order for a birthing pool. A natural birth was planned, but the levels for intervention were lower than they would be for someone not on the books of a cardiologist. This meant she would be hooked up to quite a lot of kit in the birthing suite, which was effectively an operating-theatre-equipped hospital room.

With Max predicted to arrive on Christmas Day, Sam was determined to do all she could to avoid that actually happening. She was worried about him forever having to share his birthday with the celebration of Christmas, so she was doing all the things recommended to naturally encourage a birth – going for a long walk, taking a hot bath, and finally having a spicy curry with a couple of her friends. The latter seemed to do the trick. After her hotter than usual Balti, she started having what we thought were contractions. They were well spaced out, so we remained calm, and went to bed to see what the morning would bring. We didn't get that far. Instead, Sam woke me at around 1am, saying the pains had become more regular and intense. We sat and timed them a few times, then decided to head to the hospital.

It was between two and three in the morning when we arrived. Once finally in the hands of the midwives, and the already familiar medical professionals, the experience became one of organised calm. It was a fairly lengthy labour and Max was born some 14 hours later, at around 4:15pm, delivered by ventouse suction. Samantha was exhausted by the time Max was ready to make his appearance, and the assisted method of bringing him into the world left her with a third degree tear. Yet despite these things, the birth was still very calm, I'd done my bit to make that happen, and Max was soon suckling for his first feed. I'd never seen anything so horrifically beautiful as his birth.

Max was born just three days before Christmas. Not ideal, some might say, but it did mean I got a lot of time at home with him and Sam. I'd been keeping a week of holiday in reserve to add to my week of parental leave, but with him actually arriving during the festive holidays, my parental leave and the week I'd saved to supplement it didn't actually start until the new year, meaning I had nearly a month off with my wife and son. I'd forgotten all about work, and was enjoying the togetherness of our shiny, new family unit. That was my new normal. And that fact made it difficult for me to leave my new home-life surroundings and head back to work.

I am not ashamed to say I cried the night before I went back to the office (I'm sure some of my staff were weeping too, albeit for different reasons). Our second honeymoon period was over. I'd been completely consumed by becoming a family, and the very thought of returning to work made me sad. Upon returning, I was forever distracted, and envious of my wife at home with our newborn child. This despite the fact that I know – and completely accept – that infants are pretty boring, and mostly hard work. But that's where I wanted to be. At home with the two of them, not stuck in the office making money for other people.

I muddled through until the end of July, doing just enough to justify my existence, but not really endearing myself to the managing director and owner. I'd always been selflessly ruthless at work. As an operations manager, responsible for all the site functions of our business – arranging the manufacture of systems predominantly used in the health industry – I'd been forever moving the business towards autonomy. It being a relatively small business (thirty-ish people), but with a decent turnover (£14,000,000-ish, around US$22,000,000), and as one of the business's three managers, I was always split between actual operational functions and guiding the direction of the company. My big picture work and drive for efficiency meant that the business didn't necessarily miss me if I was absent for a few days. But work really was a drag, and more of an interruption to my life than it had ever been. Hate isn't a word I like to use, but I was feeling as close to it as I ever had, and I'd worked at IKEA in my youth. So our planned holiday to the countryside was very welcome.

Samantha was happy too. Prior to having Max, we went on holiday a lot. In the previous year, our first as a married couple, we'd been on various exotic holidays. We spent a week in a catered chalet, skiing in the French Alps. The year before that, we'd got married, honeymooning in the Bahamas, and still managed foreign trips for stag dos and to be sure that Samantha had an authentic tan before we got married. But this was the first holiday Sam was taking with her baby, and her parents, and me, all together. She was extra happy.

Her planning had been meticulous as ever – researching the perfect holiday cottage, finding one in a beautiful and remote part of Somerset, yet close to the delights of a seaside resort, Weston-super-Mare. She had compiled a folder of all the activities we might enjoy as a group – where we might eat out, where we might go on a rainy day, as well as where we might 'escape' to if her parents fancied a spot of babysitting. Her planning extended to the equipment we may need with a newborn on holiday. I like to think I contributed here too. I am a big fan of things having dual purposes, particularly on holiday. It fills me with glee – and a little smugness – when I think I've introduced efficiency to our life. Like, for instance, we had a small inflatable boat, a little dinghy for our son to enjoy riding on in the sea. This also doubled up as his bath in the evening, and tripled up as a small paddling pool in the courtyard of our picturesque holiday cottage.

We were set. High chair, bouncer, the aforementioned multi-functional boat, portable DVD players, details on all the local amenities and places to visit.

I remember the drive well. You'd think a three- to four-hour car trip with an infant, to the middle of nowhere, would be hellish, but it was bliss. Our happiness was very evident. We were singing along to the radio and my iPod. Samantha even found a new song for me, one that she thought applied very aptly to her relationship with me. It was a song by No Doubt called 'Underneath It All'. Basically, Gwen Stefani sings about someone who 'underneath it all' is lovely and that she is very lucky to be with. I took a little umbrage as to why my nice qualities had to be 'underneath it all' – did I have a rubbish outer? I was playfully teased, all the while accepting that she was right, it summed me up pretty well. We took turns entertaining the boy, reading stuff and pulling faces at him. I remember having a bit of a giggle at the grandparents following, whom we'd caught a glimpse of in our rear-view mirror bickering about something or other. We speculated if that would be us in thirty years time.

After we arrived we took a bit of time to get our stuff spread around the cottage and get used to our surroundings. Sam's parents ventured out with Max to see how far Weston-super-Mare was and reported back, bringing some seaside crap they'd bought for him on the pier.

The weather was pretty good, an obsession for us Brits, even when holidaying at home. We took advantage of it and headed out for a day at a farm. I was to get very familiar with this sort of place in the future. They had a maize maze – see what they did there? – animal feeding, tractor riding, and plastic cows that you could 'milk'. Sam enjoyed milking a pretend cow. I'm not entirely sure they were intended for the adult visitors, but I guess she was acting as a proxy for our infant, who was a little too young to really take in where he was, but at least he was getting used to days out.

Sunshine continued into the afternoon. More of that horrible baby sunscreen was applied, the stuff that goes from green to invisible so you can be sure you've coated your little treasure thoroughly. And what do we do in England when the sun peeks out? We barbecue. We don't have the best climate for barbecuing, but boy, do we have an obsession with it. Charcoal was purchased, and enough raw meat to have put the farm we'd visited back in profit. Getting a bit ahead of ourselves, we bought our son his first wetsuit, ready for him to use, maybe later that year.

The grounds of our cottage were a wonderful setting for alfresco cooking and eating. I took charge of the grill. Granddad filled the boat with warm water for Max to paddle in. Sam set up some background music, Damien Rice I think, on the portable DVD. It was a lovely afternoon. Max, like the rest of us, had spent the whole day smiling. I think we all felt very lucky.

Despite being on holiday there was no deviation from the night-time routine. The paddling pool had become a bath, and Max was despatched to his travel cot beside our bed. All us adults put our feet up in the lounge. You know you are getting on well, when no one reaches for the TV remote control. It's the go-to method of occupying the mind, if only partly, in most living rooms, a good way for people to relax and not notice they are ignoring one another. This was not one of those times. This was an evening of chatter, mostly from Samantha. She didn't always hog the limelight, although she did love it. There were just times when she was feeling very chatty. It was something I did love about her. And she had so much to say that evening. She was enthused about so many things, and not just in her own life.

'I'm proud of all my friends,' she said. Friendship was important to Sam. She was loyal, part of a tight group of five girlfriends. She went through the list of their recent achievements. One had just done The Three Peaks Challenge, reaching the summit of the highest mountains in England, Scotland and Wales all in under 24 hours. Another had just got a promotion. One was about six months ahead of Sam in becoming a mother, and dealing with motherhood very well. There were lots of reasons for her to be proud, even though her loyalty and love meant these people need do nothing to impress her.

'If anything ever happened to me, I wouldn't want you to be on your own,' she said then, startling me.

'What?' I replied. 'I'm hoping that the only thing happening to you is spending more of your long life with me. And I wouldn't want to be with anyone else anyway.'

I think it was at this point she made another playful reference to 'Underneath It All'.

We went to bed very, very happy.

# 3.
# What just happened?

When Samantha died, we were the happiest of happy couples. We were our very own two-plus-one Glee Club. Our contentment, bliss and general feeling of wellbeing had never been higher. I couldn't recall a time when we had been so delighted with ourselves. Our situation felt perfect.

I am now petrified of perfect.

Our relationship had been pretty much plain sailing from day one, at least, once it started. I met Samantha during the summer of 2000, when one of my friends started dating one of hers. That relationship was moving on, and as a result the rest of us were drawn together more often.

The actual weekend I met Sam was not a good one for her. And no, before you pipe up, not because I entered her life, but because someone very dear to her was leaving it. Her granddad was gravely ill with cancer, and his bad health meant that a weekend we all had planned away together was curtailed. Sam didn't want to be far from home, and we didn't think it fair to leave her behind at such a sad time. Well, I probably did. I'd never met her, and quite fancied doing whatever we'd planned. I remember it involved drinking on a riverbank somewhere. But I accepted it wasn't the right thing to do.

Instead, I offered my house, or more accurately, my parents' house, as a sort of alternate hostel for our group over that weekend. It wasn't uncommon for me to do that, if my parents were away. We had a sizeable gaff, which included a hot tub in the garden. The weather was good, so we set about a relaxing weekend of lounging about in the tub, barbecuing (what else in the British sunshine?) and drinking. Sam came over a few times during the weekend, I think for some relief from witnessing her grandfather's painful end. Sam's periodic visits during the weekend always brought great calm to proceedings.

Now, it should be said that hot tubs and drinking are not always a safe combo. When you add the stone steps of our pantry into the mix, it can make for a sore end. I had run out of something to drink, and in my haste to retrieve another bottle from the pantry, I slipped down those rock-hard steps, landing heavily on my backside. I ended up with a very bruised behind indeed, a situation I was keen to show-off (those being apt words) to get a reaction.

We all appreciated that Sam needed us to treat her normally but respected the fact that she was going to struggle to find trivial things funny. Good job my bright purple bum was not trivial. That was the first time I made Sam laugh. Baring my bare, internally bleeding derrière to her put a temporary smile on her beautiful face and made her chuckle. A bit.

Whether it was the sight of my bottom that attracted Sam to me I don't know, but we became firm friends. We were both single, so naturally were spending time with one another, or be paired up to do things. We were our two groups' unofficial spokespeople, arranging stuff together on the phone. At least that's what I thought we were doing.

You'll have probably cottoned on by now that I am a little slow, and not always aware of what's going on around me. But apparently Sam wasn't spending time with me out of convenience. It was because she liked me.

A fact confirmed one Sunday night when she dropped me off after a trip to the cinema. She leant across from her driver's seat, whispering 'Come here', and planted a big kiss on my somewhat surprised lips.

I didn't move. Other than to get out of the car.

Sam was mortified, and I was in a daze. I was working in external sales in those days, so Sunday night usually included a trip to fill up my company car. That night I operated the petrol pump on autopilot. When I paid for my fuel, the till operator looked at me as if she knew what had just occurred, and when I got home, brushing my teeth before bedtime, I noticed that I had lipstick all over my face. Probably in the places a normal person would have moved their lips to meet Samantha's kiss.

Four days later, I was in Norfolk, where I took a call from Sam. I vividly remembering answering it: 'Hello, the girl who kissed me on the face.'

The conversation went along the lines of:

'I never knew you felt that way.'

'Really?'

'Really.'

'Oh.'

I explained that I'd been taken aback by her actions, but actually thought that was a good thing. It was because I was struggling to believe that a girl as wonderful as Samantha would be romantically interested in an imbecile like me. Did you read the bit about my bruised arse exposure, and the way I answered the phone to her? These weren't isolated incidents. But I guess she did see 'underneath it all' and liked what she'd found.

Still bemused, I muttered some clichés about jeopardising our friendship, questioning if I was even ready for a girlfriend. To some degree these were all genuine concerns, me thinking out loud, but really because I didn't think this was a conversation to be had when we were a couple of hundred miles apart. It needed to be in person.

Our friends convened again that Friday for a night out, and the minute I saw Sam I knew she was the one for me. I knew it before, but seeing her again – in rather fetching leather trousers – made all those feelings very real. In a busy city centre, I couldn't really see anybody else. I told her this, after a few honesty beers, and from that point we were together.

She never let me forget the 'four days of hell' she endured between 'that' phone call, and that night. Much later, I even tried proposing on the anniversary of the phone call so that day, and date, would have happy memories instead. But no. Those days were always in her go-to armoury when I needed admonishing for something or other.

I think starting from a point where we knew we got on, and really liked each other, made for a very sound basis for our relationship. We were very happy. We found somewhere to live and moved in together. I proposed. We got married. We had Max. We were growing happier every day. So, by that definition, probably the happiest we'd ever been was the night it all ended.

The night Sam died, I struggled to believe that all of that could be over. Lying motionless in a Weston-super-Mare hospital bed was my beautiful and lifeless wife. She was no more. I was going to have to say goodbye.

And what was I actually saying goodbye to? Even in my shocked and confused state, I quickly accepted that the body in front of me had once been that of my wife's, but that 'she' had already gone, and this body was what she had left behind. Her life had ended cruelly, and abruptly, she'd been ripped away from her – and our – happiness. There had been no chance for her to say goodbye. Was that really what I was facing now? Death is never easy, but the basic horrible reality cannot be ignored. Formalities have to be seen to.

Due to the gravity of the situation, leaving not only us but hospital staff clearly distraught, the decision was taken to close the hospital's accident and emergency unit. This meant that the place was suddenly eerily quiet, empty, apart from one other injured party and Samantha's corpse. It's horrible to talk in such terms, but that was the reality, that's what we were faced with.

I didn't want this situation and these moments to haunt me in the days and years to come. It would have been terrible if my happy memories were blighted and, worse, overridden by the images and memory of a stark medical suite and a passed Samantha. So I limited my time with 'Sam'. I said goodbye to the body, and I did this more because it was something I thought I must do rather than something I wanted, or needed, to do. In my head I knew I'd be saying goodbye to Samantha every day from then on.

Perhaps I was delaying facing the end of it all.

It was starting to dawn on me that I was going to need to deal with the practicality of the situation. There was the reality of having to tell other people of Samantha's death, but more importantly the fact that my son was going to need me to look after him.

Whilst simultaneously doubting my ability to look after him on my own, and feeling frightened about his ever-changing needs and whims, Max brought me moments of great calm. Being only seven months old, he was blissfully unaware of the chaos that had occurred around him. Looking at him sleeping in his car seat took me through a range of emotions. There was enormous sadness and grief for what he, and his mother had just lost, and worry about the future. Was I going to be able to do this on my own? Where was his stuff? When was his next feed due? How long has he been asleep in that car seat? Isn't it recommended we get him out of it after an hour?' In the aftermath of what had gone on, I genuinely didn't know the answers to these questions. I'd paid attention enough during his short life to have seen the answers to such questions before, but right now I couldn't muster them from memory. Were they still there? Was it shock preventing me from recalling them? Or had it all been erased? My panic would then be quelled by his mere presence. Looking at him, part of me couldn't help, or hope, that everything was going to be okay.

But I was scatty, unable to focus on anything for more than a few seconds at a time before being drawn to think about, or feel, something else. If I'd been any other animal than a human being (death itself a grave reminder that we really are animals ourselves), then I think I'd have been sedated. I was restless, confused, dazed, lost and occasionally panicked. Rather than climbing the walls, I was bouncing off them.

One of the feelings that I was occasionally awash with was a feeling of being grateful. Grateful to have even been lucky enough to meet Sam, and immensely grateful for our relationship and being blessed with our son.

And then feeling that it wasn't fair. I'd lost my wonderful wife, and my son his mother. And she'd lost us. But then life isn't fair. Is it?

Was I being taught a lesson?

Of all the emotions I seemed to be switching between – almost by the minute – anger was never really evident. I'm generally a laidback and placid soul. I don't like losing control, and that's what anger is to me. It's the same with excitement. I generally don't get carried away with things. Makes me sound terribly flat and emotionless, but I don't believe that's the case. I don't keep my emotions in check, I'm just in control of them, and my definition of control extends to not allowing them to consume me or be openly upset by them.

Crying was not a common thing for me, and before I met Sam I don't recall ever crying because I was overwhelmed by happiness. But that's something I experienced a lot in our time together. Not just in the headline-grabbing moments either, like  when she accepted my proposal, or when Max was born, but just being together and thinking about our tomorrow.

These 'tomorrows' were now very different. Samantha didn't have one. And we, my son and I, were facing our first without her.

Time crawled and raced. I had little idea of the hour. The rising sun meant it was morning, and my sister and Sam's brother arriving at the hospital meant another passage of time.

I was lying with my boy on a soft mat, in a sort of children's play area. He was awake, he was happy, he needed tending. A beautiful distraction, a temporary reprieve from grief, a chance to escape and indulge in a world that knew no loss, but just wondered where the next feed or nappy was coming from.

There was nothing more being at the hospital could achieve. We decided that heading home – wherever that was now – was the right thing to do. Sam's dad insisted he was up to the three-hour drive. I certainly wasn't. The thought of being in a car for that long was a scary prospect, let alone being responsible for driving one.

I sat in the back alongside Max, thinking about how extremely different our journeys to and from the cottage had been. I willed Max to sleep for most of the journey home. He couldn't have known what was going on, but he just behaved, or at least didn't need a lot of attention. Just enough to keep me occupied for a sporadic moment, taking me away from bewilderment and thoughts of Sam, into the very temporary focus of pulling funny faces, or putting a bottle in his mouth.

I didn't look out of the window much on the way home. The M5 motorway doesn't really go past a great many sights, but it was the thought of making eye contact with anonymous commuters that put me off gazing from the car's windows. We were all stunned and the journey was almost silent, a far cry from the joyous noise of our trip in the other direction.

The silence was broken by a call from the hospital's appointed coroner.

To this point, the hospital's staff had been beyond brilliant. They had dealt with Sam's situation with professionalism, and with a warmth and effort that showed they cared about what they did. They instantly cared for Samantha, and fought valiantly for her life. Sam was loved by everyone, seemingly even by those who were unable to save her life at the very end.

But the coroner was more matter-of-fact than I would have liked. I don't remember the exact details of the phone call. I was forgetting them the very instant the coroner was voicing them to me, such was my state of mind, but it wasn't pleasant.

These guys have a job to do, to deal with the dead, and I guess this would not have been an unusual phone call for them to make, telling the next of kin the procedure from this point – the technical, and somewhat graphic procedure – that follows someone dying in hospital.

I just wished he'd not made the call at that point, and not been so procedural and cold. I didn't share its contents with the rest of the car. It was for me to deal with anyway, and I saw no point in upsetting people with the details.

We arrived back at my parents' house, who'd dashed back from a holiday in Wales, and we spent a time just in silent embrace, unable to do little more than to hug and cry.

My mother, being quite religious and involved in her local church, had invited the vicar to her home. This was the woman who had married us, christened Max, and confirmed Samantha and I. She knew us.

She took me outside for a moment. She spoke about Samantha being safe, and other things I can't recall. Despite being confirmed to the Christian faith, I wouldn't class myself as religious, or a believer even, and this moment wasn't going to change that. But I was grateful for her words, and whatever you believe the rights and wrongs of religion to be, they helped, if only to distract me from what was going on back inside.

Samantha's dad was facing the prospect of having to go and tell his own mother, in her eighties, about Samantha's death. He decided this was something he must do in person. I offered to go with him, but like some things for me, it was something he had to do on his own.

My place was with my boy.

My boy.

Where is my boy?

When's his next feed?

It's time, I thought to myself, to be on top of that. Everything else can be sporadic, and happen in between these times, but my son needs me. And I need my son.

I hoped that we were going to be enough for each other.

# 4.
# Shit, I'm a single parent

On our way to hospital, there was a moment in which I accepted Samantha's, and to some extent, my own fate – the point at which all hope vanished and I accepted that my wife had died.

Holding her hand, as the paramedic I was unlikely ever to see again was administering oxygen and compressions, there was an acceptance of the situation. Amid the shock and confusion, there was that one fleeting moment of composure. I was calm, profoundly sad, but realistic enough to know that what we'd had together was gone and that things were going to be very different from now on.

Just how different, I had absolutely no idea.

Despite being able to recall this feeling of sudden isolation and responsibility I can't actually put a moment on realising: 'Shit, I'm a single parent.'

Really, for a long time from that night, for many months – to this day to some extent – my ability to focus was severely diminished. Some may argue that my previous state of mind had always been fairly aloof, that I was always prone to being distracted by something shiny, but losing Samantha had a huge bearing on my ability to concentrate on any one thing for a period of more than 30 seconds.

As a youngster, I think I'd seen the world as a very simple place. No grey areas. There was a right answer to everything, people fitted neatly into slots, and sweeping generalisations were my perceived reality of a lot of things. One of those things was of single parents.

Single parents, to my very youthful mind, were a bad thing, and not something I ever wanted to be. They weren't an evil blight on the world or anything, but more an undesirable situation, and one to be avoided. Naively, I thought of parenting solo as a situation that people get themselves into through poor decision-making, and that it wouldn't ever be something I'd have to worry about. No more thought had ever gone into it than that.

These were feelings that softened after school, as I learned and experienced more and more about the real world. I opened my mind more to the situations of others instead of not automatically deeming one situation to be worse or inferior to another.

However, both Samantha and I were lucky enough to be born into families fitting the traditional mould, with a mum and dad who had been together forever, married and each yielded two children, a boy first, then a girl. That was our normal and we were trying to emulate it, recreating similar picture perfect environments for our own children.

With Samantha having a congenital heart condition, I'd envisaged being left on my own at some point. But I'd always imagined that point to be in my ripe old age, when I'd been reduced to a shuffling pensioner, moaning at having to breathe for myself and the general inadequacies of all the younger folk (basically me, but older). It wasn't something I looked forward to – eventually having no one to listen to my bleating – but I imagined having got to that point in our lives, we would both be grateful for a lifetime together, and critically our children would no longer, practically, need us.

That dream was shattered, and at 28 years old I was abruptly widowed, and made a single parent, in one fell swoop.

I was still reluctant to accept that term for my situation, for a multitude of reasons. It didn't get near to the whole story quick enough, it implied a time-share parenting situation and it, in part, also suggested that I was available for a relationship. Introducing anyone as 'single' encourages the assumption that they are seeking a relationship. I was most definitely not. The thought was abhorrent to me at that point. At that time in my life, not even Britney Spears or Martine McCutcheon (long-time members on my 'list') could have scored dates with me.

Having a tag like 'single parent', or a tag of any kind, takes away the individuality of your situation. Any feelings you have of being in a unique place are quickly eroded. I was just 'one of them'.

And what was 'one of them?' A lone parent? A widowed dad? What was being a single dad going to mean? How was it going to work? Do blokes even do that? This is going to screw us both up, isn't it, me and Max? I'm going to ruin my boy, and myself in the process, aren't I?

Trying not to panic, I tried to contemplate if I was equipped to cope with my beautiful boy and all his infant demands.

I was a man who had asked the following question during a baby-bathing demo at one of our parenting classes: 'You look like you need three hands. Why can't we just shower them?'

I can't remember all my faux pas at these sessions but, seemingly impervious to feelings of embarrassment, I asked a series of questions that brought about a few giggles and probably derision from the other attendees. I'm sure some of them already feared for my child's upbringing, and that was when I was going to be playing a supporting role to the main carer. Now I was alone. Alone and in charge.

Were these people right? Would I have the first clue?

Luckily for my son, I'd already come a long way from my narrow-minded youth, from a person who perhaps would have let gender dictate what someone could or couldn't do, to now being someone who'd continually ask: Why not? As an example, I'd asked my sister to be the best man at our wedding, not because I didn't have some good friends to choose from, but because if she'd been born as my brother, I'd not have hesitated in asking her. Why should it be any different because she was a woman? Plus I'd developed a slightly rebellious resolve not to accept that it was ever impossible for me to do what I wanted to, regardless of convention.

Despite my laid-back and somewhat jovial nature, including my behaviour at our parenting classes, there was often a serious reason why I would play the fool. There can be a benefit in asking questions you think you know the answer to. As new parents, I was surprised how much we were just expected to know, so the very beginning seemed the right place to start. I was asking 'stupid' questions because I wanted answers, reassurance, and my thinking was that a million stupid questions were better than making one stupid mistake.

Like right after the birth of my son, or soon after we'd spent some time in a collective cuddle, I was charged with clothing him for the first time.

'There'll be a vest in the baby bag,' I was told.

I spent two minutes looking for what I thought a vest was – a sleeveless T-shirt. There was no such thing in the bag. There was a cotton leotard thing with no legs, but not a 'vest'. Finally, holding it aloft, I asked, 'Do you mean this?' I was met with wry smiles, and how-can-you-not-know-that looks.

Asking questions is never going to be a bad thing. And if you ask a question with sufficient confidence, or follow it with a statement to show that you understand, it quickly subdues any ridicule.

I think the feeling of not knowing anything as a new parent is heightened for a man. I don't recall a single conversation I had with either of my parents about the practicalities of parenting, or how it was for them. I'm pretty sure, like lots of women, my wife had a very good idea of how it had been for her parents, and had a more intimate and practical knowledge of the rearing of young ones.

There's also the general fact that I don't pay attention to something until I have to. I'd had a few friends that had become parents before us, but I'd not really paid proper attention to what that meant. I more just observed the difference in our interactions with them – as in, we didn't have them anymore. I'm sure my friends and work colleagues would have shared lots of information with me about raising children, but before it had any relevance I would have consigned that information to the bin rather than memory.

That changed though, and throughout Samantha's pregnancy I became a better listener to men who'd become dads, keeping my ears pricked for gems of information, occasionally stoking the fire of confrontation when I found two dads with differing views. Dummies/pacifiers always seem to divide people, as does when a baby should start sleeping in their own room. A well placed 'That's not what such and such said' would often cause a bit of a fracas and friction – for my entertainment – but also force these dads to put more meat on the bones of their arguments. I listened to it all.

While men do talk about children (surprised you there, haven't I?), we do so often in general terms, more about the bigger picture than the nitty-gritty. We would make a comment about whose job changing nappies is, or how much of a pain it is, rather than about techniques or the best cream for nappy rash. But as a sole parent, these were things I was going to need to know.

One observation I had made of some fathers was that they weren't completely comfortable when left alone in charge of their own children. I didn't want to feel the same way. It was a selfish attitude in some ways, but I didn't ever want to be in a position of having to rely on others for the care of my son. The idea of not being able to look after my child, regardless of whether I was going to have to, made me nervous. Even though the plan was always that I would be the breadwinner and Samantha the main care provider, despite me knowing she'd do a brilliant job and being convinced it was the right way to set our family up, I didn't want to be in a position of not being equipped to be the care provider should I ever need to take my turn.

I didn't know at the time. How could I? I'd always envisaged Samantha's absences would be fleeting, but thought taking a very hands-on role would pay dividends, if only on the practical front.

When Samantha had recovered from childbirth, I encouraged her to take a well-deserved trip away. After all she'd been through, I thought she more than deserved it. Plus it would give me the opportunity to spend a period in absolute sole charge of my child. It would be good for all of us, I thought. Samantha made plans to go off to Sweden to visit a friend and I was in charge, despite the offers of only-too-willing grandparents to take care of Max that weekend.

It took a great deal of persuasion to get Samantha to go away, and concentrate on only herself and her friends for a weekend. I think all new parents feel a degree of separation anxiety, and she was no different, but I was warmed by the fact that she never did question my ability to care for our child. Not that I'd given her any reason to doubt my ability, but

I'd witnessed many mothers who were not prepared to leave their other halves in charge of the children for too long.

So now, faced with permanently caring for my son alone, I didn't doubt my ability from a practical point of view. In fact, armed with a why-the-hell-not attitude, I was convinced I was able to do it. But was I right? As a man, what was I missing? Apart from a vagina, obviously. Women do this in their sleep, don't they? They are built to do it, they have a proven maternal instinct. But how many men do it?

I didn't know. Nor could I think of a single man I knew that was child rearing on his own.

Phrases such as 'Only a mother' and 'Mums know best' seemed instantly haunting. I was already imagining my dysfunctional future child, unable to relate to anyone else, to even demonstrate a glimmer of empathy with anyone or anything, and forever saddled with the lazy excuse of, 'Well, his mum died when he was a baby.'

Would he be better off without me? Who was I doing this for – me or him?

These were the questions that would fly around my head as my focus flitted from one thing to another. Grief was draining my confidence, and self-doubt was an emotion I would feel and deal with regularly, even if I did not show or share it.

I knew I had to believe in myself. Samantha always had, and she was no fool. Her death, if nothing else, was going to inspire me to be the best bloody parent I could be.

The best damn single parent the world had ever seen.

End of.

# 5.
# Going home

Where was home now?

About twelve months after we'd become a couple, Samantha and I decided that we wanted to live together. Both in our early twenties and still enjoying the home comforts that our parents provided, we decided it would be a good time for us to get on the property ladder. It would be good for our independence, good for our parents' collective sanity, the right move for our relationship and seemingly financially sensible as we could still afford to make the move at a time when house prices were beginning to soar. It was not a now or never moment, but certainly a 'now or it will be more expensive tomorrow' one.

Samantha worked for a bank so that was where we started for a mortgage. Despite a healthy joint income, meaning we could borrow more, we set a relatively conservative budget, a very much living-within-our-means limit to what we'd commit to paying back. I don't know if this was motivated by thoughts of the future, of starting a family and eventually surviving on one wage, or on it not working out and one of us still being able to afford any property we bought on our own. For me, it was much more of the former. For Sam, I'll let you decide.

Then it was time to sit down and decide on where we wanted to live, and what sort of property we were looking for. The areas we both lived in as children would not be described as idyllic. In fact, Jeremy Clarkson, bless him, once described the town I grew up in as the worst place in the world. That's unjustified and untrue (he can't have been everywhere, right?) but it certainly wasn't a salubrious oasis in the very busy middle of England. Like a lot of the suburban areas of the West Midlands, neighbouring streets can be very different, good and bad. So we created a short list of the streets we would be prepared to live in, near each of the areas we already knew. We decided we didn't want to live in a new property – it must be one with character, and generally more space. We'd need three bedrooms.

Properties were on and off the market very quickly then, so it was a case of keeping eyes peeled when the property pages were published each week, as well as spotting 'for sale' boards going up outside properties in the streets on our list. Which is what happened with the property we eventually bought. It was the second property we saw, and we both loved it. And pretty soon we owned it, too – a house on Park Lane, no less (though sadly not the one on the Monopoly board).

There was some friction at the beginning, as we both went from barely raising a finger living with our parents, to sharing the responsibilities of having our own home. I did most of the cooking, Sam did most (all) of the cleaning, both of us believing that we had it harder than the other. Ironing was the one chore we could never agree on, so that became the sole task we outsourced, paying someone else to make our clothes flat.

We got stuck into home improvements. My dad and I put in a new bathroom. Sam's brother helped take out the fireplace, install a new lintel and create a cool space. The downstairs floorboards were sanded and varnished. Samantha and I did a great job of that, apart from varnishing ourselves out of house. As we stood admiring our glorious real wood floor, it took us a little while to realise that we couldn't walk on it for a few hours, and actually, as we were now stood in our garden, we were locked out. We had to call parents to rescue us and let us back into our own home.

There were many painting sessions, re-tiling, tearing out the old, putting in the new. We put a lot of effort into that home. It was definitely mine and Sam's, there was no mistake about that.

But soon it was going to be our son's first home too.

During Samantha's pregnancy my home office became the nursery, not that Max was going in there straight away. Max came back to our home from hospital for the first time on Christmas Eve, so the first morning we all woke up together at our Park Lane home was Christmas Day.

In his very early days I made a video diary of what was going on – how well his mother was coping with him and her recovery, what he'd been up to and who'd seen him. I've not watched 'Daddy's Log' much since, and Max is yet to see it, but it includes lovely footage of our home, and the snowy Christmas scene outside when our boy was a newborn. There's a lot of love in that footage. There was a lot of love in that home. But we were already beginning to outgrow it.

We were thinking about space and schools. From a professional point of view my salary had risen to match, and then better, that of our collective income when we first bought our house. It meant we could afford a larger mortgage, even on just my salary, and we were of the belief that we'd want the space for ourselves, as well as any more children we might have.

The housing market had stalled somewhat, but we found a house we both liked, in a leafier neighbourhood, and critically one owned by a builder who was prepared to take our property in a part-exchange deal. As we ventured off on our first family holiday to Somerset, the deal was almost done. We were just waiting on a single outstanding search, and a phone call confirmation from the builder's solicitor.

I believe that phone call came the morning after my wife had died. And whilst I was never going to honour the deal to move, it signified to me that our time, our happy time at Park Lane, was done.

I chose to move back in with my parents.

I've heard many people say derogatory things about moving 'back home'. Many of my friends who'd gone off to university said how difficult it was to move back in with parents, or that it would be an option they'd only consider if faced with living on the street. Similarly, when friends' relationships had broken down, they often spoke about the negatives of having to retreat to their family home.

I had my reservations about going home, and did consider staying in our marital abode. But I didn't want to risk tarnishing the happy memories of that place with miserable, lonely and desolate ones of Max and I living there without Samantha. Park Lane had been brilliant for us as a couple, and continued to be for us as a young family, but if things had gone to plan its time would have been up anyway. We'd almost physically moved on, and now I saw this as right – to try to cement the memories we'd made there, rather than blight them.

My parents' house is huge. It's actually two large semi-detached houses that have been adapted into a single home. I guess in theory it's an eight-bedroom house, but during its time as our family home for us – my parents and us, their two kids – it was two three-bedroom houses separated by a large playroom.

My sister Emma and I effectively lived on one side, our parents on the other. This became increasingly handy for all of us when we became teenagers, and the noise, goings-on and crowd of that age group descended on the house.

It only meant that now, once again, the house could informally be split into two: a side for Max and myself, and a side for my parents. Furniture was collected from my old home and pretty soon we each had our own set up. We had our own lounge and playroom, as well as a bedroom each. I again decided against returning to old ground, taking up residence in what had been my sister's room.

I am so grateful to my parents. Not only for taking me in, but for recognising that I needed my own space, as much as possible. I would always claim to have a good, and close, relationship with my parents, but I think one of our weaknesses, perhaps, has been an inability to share our feelings, to see things easily from the other's point of view. We'd not been fans of change, or discussing them with one another.

The reasons for moving back home were not born out of needing help with my child – in fact, I was clinging to being Max's dad as my new identity – but out of not wanting to go back to my old house, and my parents provided the best and most obvious option. I thought it was critical for Max, and also for me, to be the main care-provider. It would have been all too easy to watch others take care of my boy while I moped and felt sorry for myself. In fact, no, scratch that. It would have been understandable and excusable, I'm sure, but it wasn't something that I could do. As unfocused as I was, I had an inner drive to continue to be the parent I'd always been. Watching others take care of my son would have been torture, and perhaps have added to my torment, introducing feelings of inadequacy and being no use at all to Max, along with all the other crap in my head.

At a time of immense grief and sadness, with many of my body's functions shutting down, becoming numb or only working momentarily, there was an inherent instinct to continue to care for my son. I could be distracted by different events and thoughts, but come feed time, change time, bath time or bedtime, I was right on point, snapping straight out of my state of distraction to attention. Despite what had happened the routine remained constant. I never missed a beat.

We'd parented with a lot of love, but also with as firm a hand as we could muster. Feeding was regular, as was the list of banned things. Naptime was scheduled and to be taken as prescribed, as was bedtime and our baby being in his own room.

Driven by a feeling that I needed to keep my son close, desperately wanting him to feel loved and comforted, we shared a bed for a number of nights – I don't recall how many. I didn't want to be alone in the still of night, either. Amongst the many things Sam had been to me, I'd lost my sleeping partner of the last five or six years, and I wasn't ready to try sleeping on my own yet. Plus, sleep was minimal for me. It was more a case of lying there with all sorts of thoughts going through my head, almost willing my son to wake and interrupt me, rescuing me from them. I'm not sure there's ever been anyone so grateful for a crying baby in the early hours of the morning.

Being back home wasn't without its difficulties. It was important for me to remember that, as hard as it was for me to go through the loss of a wonderful spouse, my parents had watched their child – me – go through the pain of it all too. They both loved Samantha. She'd formed special relationships with both of them, particularly with my dad. My old man has never been renowned for his openness, compassion, tolerance and warmth. He was generally someone perceived as the opposite – cold and grumpy. Sam saw through all that and developed a very good friendship with him. There were things they'd share that perhaps he'd not find easy discussing with other people.

As part of her routine, Wednesday had become Sam's 'Newbold' day. She'd spend the morning at a local playgroup with my mother, then as my mum headed off to volunteer at a local hospital in the afternoon, Samantha and Max would spend the rest of the day in the company of my dad. Through regular interaction like this, they'd all become incredibly close.

My mum and dad were devastated by the loss of Sam. They would miss her terribly themselves, but they also mourned for the effect it had on me, and the loss their first grandchild had suffered. Their grief actually helped me take my mind off my own woes occasionally. I knew they were both hurting, and I understood the impact Sam's death had had on them, too. I tried to be the shoulder for them to rest on, as reluctant as they were to let me. I think that's one of the unwritten rules of how to be a good parent – to be there for your child, not the other way around.

Another difficulty for parents is to accept that sometimes there is nothing you can do, and, in fact, doing nothing can actually be the best thing for your child.

I was striving to prove myself as Max's dad. He was for me to deal with. One of my fears was that by letting people assist me too much, Max would become confused by being passed from pillar to post, or worse, in some way harbour the feeling that he wasn't wanted, or loved, or that he was an inconvenience. Which could not be further from the truth. I could not have wanted him more; selfishly, I needed him. He was an unwitting rock to me in my darkest hours, a beacon of light, someone who, if I was only near, I could see hope, feel love and warmth, and experience a sense of calm. He was like the opposite of Kryptonite. He still is today.

But I think, in part, my need to take complete care of my son, and doing so within my parents' home, left them feeling a little useless and lost. I knew I was being relatively insensitive to this, but I judged it to be more important to concentrate on what I was doing rather than to make changes and take actions that would have been more about making them feel better.

I'm sure I got on their nerves, and was definitely difficult to approach. I would spurn their offers of help, even be rude (yes, me) on occasion. I treated their home as a hotel and would get annoyed if they even poked their heads around the door of our lounge. It was unfair, but I guess this was me venting in a way, and also a result of any insecurity I had about establishing myself as Max's main carer. I wanted him to know, I wanted everyone around to know, that I was his dad, and with his mother gone, I was going to be the one looking after him. No one else.

Living with my folks had its practical benefits. It did mean I could pop out for things if I needed to. I was well fed and watered, leaving me able to concentrate on looking after Max, but it was clear to me that living with my parents could only be a temporary thing. It was not going to work for me as a permanent place to live. I had no idea how long 'temporary' was going to be, or where Max and I might end up living, but I knew the current situation could not go on forever.

All our relationships probably suffered a bit as a result of me moving in with my parents. Not that I feel any guilt – and neither should my folks. Of course I found it difficult to surrender my independence, and it must be equally hard to let others come and go as they please in your own home. I know that in some families, many generations live together. Some are not lucky enough to have any other choice. It brings some closer together, and really works for them, but my worry was that the longer it went on for us, the bigger the danger that it would ultimately drive us apart.

# 6.
# What about work?

When Samantha and I met, we were both employed in the lovely world of sales. She was a seller of finance for a high-street bank, and I was an external salesman working in a business-to-business environment. Though both in sales, these were very different jobs, for very different people. Sam was using her charms on the public to match their needs, and convincing them to use the financial products her bank had on offer. She was very good at her job, though not necessarily in the eyes of the bank, who would have liked her to be more aggressive, selling what she could rather than what the customers might need. In the global financial crisis and meltdown of recent years, I smirk a little at the thought that my late wife would have been very 'told you so' about it all.

Sam was very much a people person. Me, not so much. I've never really had the patience.

My sales job was dissimilar to Sam's, as I was selling to manufacturing businesses, generally dealing with a combination of buyers, designers and engineers. It was a commercial role, in which the technical part of it – knowing the products and the solutions they could enable – played a much bigger aspect.

Sam's growing discomfort with the bank's aggressive selling motives led her to move over to the service side of the business, where she was in charge of improving the customers' experience of visiting the bank. It was not without its own stresses and ridiculous constraints, but it was a role she was very good at, and one she was less reluctant to get out of bed to go and do.

What it did mean though, was that her career – in terms of pay – stalled a little. She was still earning a reasonable wage for someone of her age, but was no longer on the progressive sales job route that would have meant more money for her as well as the bank.

At the same time my job, was changing too. Just like Sam, I'd stumbled into what I was doing rather than following a calling. My interests, even as a child, had always been wide-ranging, and critically, forever changing. I've been asked a lot of times: 'What did you want to grow up to be when you were a kid?' My son asks this a lot, probably as I've never been able to muster much of an answer.

As the eldest child in a nuclear family, I had a dad that had always been the breadwinner. During my childhood, he was generally always there, but clearly very, very stressed by his job. He was someone who would take a good while to zone out and relax, but he always eventually found the time to be with us, and I never felt like he compensated by buying flash stuff. He didn't need to.

My mum had also been successful. She'd been to a good university, and ended up in teaching. But during our formative years, she took a break from full-time work to look after us. My sister was well underway at school, and myself nearly in secondary school, before my mum got another teaching job – at the high school both her children would eventually attend, no less. ('DOES YOUR MOTHER NEED TO COME TO SCHOOL WITH YOU?' I remember one music teacher bellowing at me, when I showed up a bit bedraggled after a Phys Ed class, with my tie not done up properly. How else was I going to answer other than 'Yes, sir'?)

My mum and dad provided a sound, very traditional family environment. My mother was generally in charge of looking after us kids, as my dad went out and earned the 'serious' money. Mum's income was more the budget that as a trio, myself, my mum and my sister would play with. And although mum worked, as a teacher her holidays mirrored ours, so she was always with us, or at least organising us when we were at home.

Everyone in our family worked, and worked hard. So I guess I just planned to do the same.

When my A-levels finished, I started my first full-time job immediately. I worked as a pipe-fitter's mate for the summer, whilst applying for jobs I thought were going to be better suited to me. I took up a commercial apprenticeship before the onset of winter (and a cold building site), enjoying a couple of years and promotions with a firm I was quickly outgrowing, then moved on to start another career selling for someone else. It was a field in which I had no experience, the company's main areas of work being hospital and care, selling the electrical bits that make hospital beds, hoists and medical benches go up and down. In fact, as they wheeled out the obligatory first interview question – 'What do you know about the company?' – I had to resort to a joke . 'Well, I knew how to get here. Can we start with that?'

It ended up being a very good match, as it was a company that was growing with me, rather than working against me. I was promoted, or took on a new responsibility, almost every twelve months. After seven years with them, and at the time of my wife's death, I was one of three managers running a now more than 30-employee business with a turnover in the several millions. But still – was it what I was born to do?

I'd actually semi-achieved my original aim. After seeing how stressed my dad's high-powered job made him, all I really wanted was a well-paid job with no stress. I was comfortably close to earning a six-figure salary, and my job would rarely keep me up at night or away from home for too long. In that respect I was lucky, but I still was not excited by it, and did it essentially because of the benefits, rather than a love of the job.

Before my wife got pregnant I'd say I had represented true value for money as an employee. I worked hard without really every going above and beyond, and strived to improve all the aspects of the business I had control of. Through my actions we became more efficient, profitable and cash-rich. But my focus was severely thrown during Sam's pregnancy. With me needing more time out to attend the almost weekly medical appointments at her side, I would have to admit to drifting a little. I was always there for important meetings, my staff never complained about me being inaccessible, and I completed regular tasks like reports for the parent company, but in my mind I was coasting, probably for the first time in my professional career.

Throughout my working life I'd periodically ponder on my direction, whether I was in the right field, if I was really enjoying what I did, pretty much coming to the same conclusion each time – the money I was earning facilitated other parts of my life I did enjoy, plus I was good at what I was doing (or at least found it easy) and I couldn't really come up with anything else I desperately wanted to do.

I never got a sense of pride from my job. I would rarely talk about it at home or with friends. I was driven enough to be the best at what I was doing at the particular time, but didn't care as much as others about getting to the top. I think I am wired a little differently to some men. My dad included. We'd had discussions, my dad and I, probably at times when I'd got itchy feet at work, or was looking for the next challenge. We differed in the fact that, like many people, he got a sense of satisfaction from a job well done, and saw some value in being responsible for a large budget, a company's direction and people's jobs. He liked being important.

I never got it. To me – then – a job was very much a job. If you didn't turn up to do yours, ultimately someone else would. Not just for us pen-pushers, but for brain surgeons, pilots and chefs too. I'd ask myself: Is what someone does for a living impressive in itself? Not really. I have always been more impressed, and envious, of people doing things because they love doing them. If they happen to be incredibly well paid and successful too, great, but to have a calling, a passion – that's when I really admire people.

At the point Samantha died, I'd been the breadwinner, which meant for the first time in my life I was somewhat morally obligated to work and financially provide for others. It would not have been easy for me to say: 'You know what, I think I'm going to join the circus.' We were no different to most middle-Britain families, part of the rat race, earning to live, living to earn. And because of the security, stability and relative luxuries my salary afforded us, any quibble I had about not really enjoying my job was quickly put to bed.

As we'd been on holiday, it took a little time for the news of my wife's death to filter back to my boss. I think my dad actually broke the news, or certainly was the first of us to speak to him. A few days later I had a phone call with my superior, the managing director of the company, but we spoke more out of courtesy to each other, him offering his sympathies, assurances that I wasn't under pressure to return to work and me – well, I'm not really sure what I said.

The truth is, I think I'd already decided I couldn't go back to work, or to that job. My son needed me, and I needed him.

I'm not sure I said these thoughts out loud, and if I did, they would not have been fully formed. It was very difficult at the time to make any sort of decision, other than when to feed, change or bathe my son. We had things like the funeral to sort out, and then there was what to do with the house.

I think there was a certain expectation that after a period of grieving, my best and most obvious course of action would be to go back to work and have Max taken care of by his grandparents. From the outside, I think that was the solution that made the most sense to other people. I had a 'good' job, the grandmothers had the experience of raising children, and the time. Add to that the general perception that men need to work, because they're not really built to look after children. 'You'll need something to do,' people would say to me. I quietly agreed, knowing that when they meant gainful employment, I was thinking about the raising of my little boy.

If things had gone to plan, I would have continued to work. Sam may have gone back in a part-time capacity if she'd found being a full-time mum a little tedious, but more likely she was looking at a professional hobby. She would have enjoyed training or learning to do something like dressmaking, which would have facilitated a grown-up element in her daily life, as well as a possible revenue stream.

But in all our plans, Max was at the centre. His care was the all-important thing. We didn't want to lose our identities, and would have had other things in our lives, but he was the point around which it all revolved. It was a plan we were both happy with, and I saw no reason why its essence shouldn't remain now.

It was difficult to think too far ahead, to the future. I needed time to get this absolutely right. I knew I was in no fit state to return to work. It would probably have been dangerous for myself, my son, and probably my employees, to have returned in such a numb and bewildered condition. So I didn't.

I tried to focus, one bit at a time, at getting this decision right. And right for everyone. And by everyone, I meant for Max and I. Before his mother died, he was set for a life of great stability, to be showered with love and attention. Of all the things I was having to let go of, I wasn't prepared for that to be one of them.

An increasing number of doubts were raised by some of the people closest to me, and I always appreciated them. There were some ill-judged comments by people who mistakenly thought I gave any weight to their opinion, but generally I appreciated the honesty of people around me. Close friends had put themselves through the pain of imagining being in the same situation themselves, and what decisions they might make, and their questioning me was good. It challenged my mind, and got me thinking about the impact my choice might have.

There were financial considerations. I needed a revenue stream, though I knew through previous financial prudence, and not needing to spend a great deal now, that I was afforded time before that would be a real issue.

Scenarios concerning the possible negatives for my professional career, the impact on my CV of giving up a job, that sort of thing, didn't really worry me at all. Sam's death had put my professional existence into proper context. Indeed, my thoughts were occasionally drifting to finding a proper calling, something I could do for myself, that would reward me, not only financially, but through self-actualisation.

While the decision I was working towards making felt very final, it didn't have to be that way. These were going to be unchartered waters for me. I was only guessing how I'd cope with the care of my young son, and what stresses and strains it would put on my already heavy heart.

My decision-making had always been pretty sound. Even when I may have taken a wrong turn, I did with good intentions, and with all of what I could know in advance considered. I learned from my mistakes as I went, and learned quickly.

So perhaps here I was being presented with an opportunity. My wife had died, our previous family life with her, but now, right in front of me, was my flesh and blood in need of someone to look after him, to be at his side as he learned to walk, as he learned to speak, as he cut and lost his first tooth. That someone could be me.

My wife had from the outset been a little envious of the connection I'd made with my boy. I think as a man, a father, there's part of us that never really learns to grow up, the inner child that at times finds it easier to get into the mindset of children. To play. To act daft. To spout nonsense. To act without fear of what others might think or say. This would be a chance to grow that bond even stronger.

Samantha had also been sympathetic to the short period of time when I would be working, while she was with Max all day. He'd be in a great mood all day, only to be tired in the early evening, resist his dinner from me, and then cry as much water into his bath as was already in it. 'You get the worst of him,' she'd say.

Now I could be the one seeing the good stuff.

I wasn't looking at this as the 'up side' of becoming a widower. It was just the fact that, with all the shit, there was also going to be some newfound joy. My boy represented hard work, and a steep learning curve, but he also represented hope and purpose.

My purpose.

# 7.
# Taking counsel

There are stages to grief, apparently. I would have to perform a Google search to tell you what they are precisely, but I believe they include things like acceptance, anger, shock, letting go, depression and rebuilding.

Given that I had lost my wife, it might have been a reasonable thing to – as I no doubt accept it is – to research and read about grief, learn about its possible stages and how to best handle the grieving process, or even just what to expect. There are plenty of wise people in the world who will have studied and theorised in equal measure. They will have developed lots of resources and guides for dealing with loss, to aid the rest of us. I am positive there are many brilliant works, from many brilliant minds, that could help people in their hours of need and desperation.

But the big thing I found when dealing with Samantha's death was how numb and unfocused it made me immediately afterwards. I can't claim to have been the most alert person beforehand, but I have always felt sharp, in a permanent state of standby, able to step up, take charge and focus on a job that needed doing at any given moment. When Sam died this ability seemed to die with her. I went from being able to pick things up quickly to a steady state of empty. All the time it felt like I'd just been to a very loud music concert. My mind was in that weird state you get for a couple of hours after listening to loud music, like being underwater, not hearing anything, anybody, or any thought clearly.

Reading and learning about anything at that time was immensely difficult. I became incredibly reliant on others for anything other than looking after my baby boy, or learning about what he may need.

There is so much a parent has to know and consider, but a baby's development is generally slow, and changes that may seem massive to parents are really only minor taken one at a time. In my case, it meant that I could focus temporarily on these, and task myself only with thinking about and researching my boy's latest development or upgrade.

He started crawling just days after his mother's death, but that's the first thing I can recall he started to do differently. He'd been showing himself willing in the time before her passing, spending an increasing amount of time lying on his tummy and pushing his head up. Sam and I had studiously read up on how we could help and encourage this next stage of his mobility. We'd garnered ideas like putting him on his stomach more often, laying things just outside his reach, and thinking about footwear with better grip.

We'd also have one eye on the next stage. Once crawling, we knew, he'd be off, and have access to all areas his four paws could drag him to. He'd soon be able to pull hot drinks from coffee tables, go and inspect things up close, experience the glory of putting things in plug sockets and tasting any stray item he found. We were aware of these things, and could plan to adapt his environment to better suit his newfound abilities in advance.

It was relatively easy for me, at least within my new, somewhat limited capabilities, to recall what we'd already learnt, and to find and retain small pockets of information that were useful to me as a parent, and my boy as a developing infant. For anything more complex, like dealing with Samantha's estate, my house sale or my work situation, I needed help and guidance, which was generously provided by my family. My dad was incredibly helpful and thoughtful. I annoy him at the best of times with my lack of attention to detail, but he was incredibly patient with me, and at the very least hid any frustration as we went about dealing with Sam's death and estate.

The point I am trying to make is that it wasn't the right time for academic study about my grief. To have picked up a book about loss at that stage would have been counterproductive. I'd have only got annoyed at my inability to understand the text properly and then panicked about not being in the best place to deal with each of its supposed stages. I'd be worried about getting things wrong, and further hindering myself, and possibly my son, in the process.

That's just one reason I wouldn't have been inclined to go down the 'study to recover' route. I've never been shy of study – I continued my formal education alongside work right up to the point at which I was widowed, for example – but for me the purpose of any academic endeavour has to be beyond clear, its benefits incredibly convincing, and to be as specific as possible. Of course, here I could see the point – that there was a benefit to me understanding the grieving process, and that it might be an easier road for me to travel should I know what to expect on the way. Reading about the experiences of others, and the findings of researchers and studies, would all definitely have had merits.

But there's also the cynical, arrogant part of me that is convinced I am best equipped to deal with things myself, and that following anyone else's pattern – no matter how esteemed they might be – couldn't possibly be the best way for me to go. And isn't grief different for everyone anyway?

I was going to handle things as they came. On my own. My way.

So how well do you think the suggestion of grief counselling went down?

After a couple of weeks of being off work, and still being in the kind of crippled state that prevented me from returning to it, I was in the position of having to prove that fact. Compassionate leave can only be expected to last a certain amount of time, and I'm not someone who is a fan of the inconclusive or ill defined. So I visited my GP to explain what had happened and what I guess were the symptoms as a result – the lack of focus, the drifting, the clouded mind, my struggle with emotions, the unpredictable sleep patterns, my concerns, stresses and occasional panics about accepting my new now, and thoughts about the future.

It was clear to my doctor that I wasn't in a fit state to return to work, that it was a good idea that I was in regular contact with him, so he could monitor my progress on medical grounds. At first I think I had weekly appointments scheduled with my doctor, at the second of which he suggested grief counselling. Any normal person, in any normal situation would probably have guessed he would. It would indeed be good practice to do so. But my addled brain hadn't seen it coming, and only really started to consider it once the doctor made the suggestion.

It surprised me that I didn't dismiss it straight out of hand. The old me would have taken such a suggestion as an insult, a derogatory slight suggesting that I wasn't strong enough to deal with the situation on my own. Counselling, pfft. Who needs that? It's for wimps and the weak, isn't it? I'm neither of those things. I don't need to talk about stuff. What good would that do anyone anyway?

But now, I was at least listening. I did wonder if it was because I no longer had the stomach for a row about it with my doctor. Was standing up for myself something of my past? Could I no longer be bothered to be opinionated? The world would be relieved, but it meant my attitude would have changed demonstratively.

No – I knew deep down that I would always be up for a fight when I deemed it necessary. But this wasn't one of those times. The doctor, who'd probably had a lot of experience dealing with people affected by loss, and had seemed genuine and diligent enough to have done some research between our meetings, was someone I needed to listen to.

I went back to my parents and told them what he'd suggested, which was met with a hesitant and collective silence. I think my parents both wondered what was going to come out of my mouth next, and thought best to let me say whatever it was, before they were drawn into saying anything or giving an opinion.

'I'm going to think about it,' I said.

There was actually no guarantee that counselling of any type would be made available to me via the National Health Service. In my questions about what may actually happen if I agreed to it, I was rather surprised to discover that my GP was limited in what he could do or recommend for me. While it had never been a consideration that I would need formal medical help to deal with grief, I was surprised at the lack of critical, funded mechanisms available to help folks deal with losses. There was no specific department at the doctor's or the hospital, no specialist available in grief counselling. I later learnt that they have a resource that deals with people believed to be in danger of physically harming themselves. But that is seen as a last resort, and a preventative for avoidable suicides, rather than anything else.

In fact, I discovered that all my doctor wanted to do was write a letter recommending that I be counselled. This letter would be sent to a voluntary organisation, called Cruse Bereavement Care, who would appraise my situation against other recent cases and then assign me resources should they have them available and think me a suitable case for a volunteer's time.

After discussing it a little with my parents and my sister, or at least using them as a sounding board, I decided that I had nothing to lose, and really should have no objections to it. It would act, at the very least, as more medical proof to make the case for my inability to return to work.

I wasn't embarrassed about going to counselling. I had much bigger things to worry about than what people might have thought. Sam's death had put a great deal into perspective, and part of me was intrigued by what the counselling sessions may yield. As a sceptic of the notion that talk could be a tool for development or healing, I was someone to be won over. I'm sure some would have been surprised that I was open to the suggestion at all, no matter how valid it was. I think some folks would just think it an incredibly unlikely route for me to take.

So the doctor sent his letter and I waited to see if Cruse Bereavement Care would deem me worthy of their precious time. Half of me hoped they would, the other hoped that it wasn't a process I would have to go through. Was I daunted about sharing my feelings with a stranger? Yes, no doubt. Generally I say what I believe, and what I come up with is more often based on logic than sentiment. It is sometimes misinterpreted as being insensitive, but I don't agree, I am sensitive to people and how they feel, but don't think that sympathy is always the best course of action.

Which was potentially part of the problem I envisaged with grief counselling. I really didn't need anyone to feel sorry for me. There was an army of people capable of that to call upon should I feel it necessary, but ultimately it's a pointless and often unproductive exercise. It does feel nice when someone sympathises with your plight, but what does it actually achieve other than a pause in your shit status quo?

I remember back in my early days of working in an office environment, one of the women I worked with, probably in her thirties at the time, lost her dad. After a few days off she came back to work. All the departments had different start times, even though we worked in the same office, and she was amongst the group that arrived last, which meant the office was generally full of people whenever she first walked in. It must have been an intimidating prospect to think she had to face all her work colleagues in one go. Right on time, she wandered in, not entirely with the vigour and confidence she usually did, as you'd expect. The first person she had to walk past, the accounts manager, and a man renowned for his lack of people skills, without hesitation said, 'Oh, hello Annie, sorry to hear your dad died.'

I kid you not.

She didn't make it to her desk. Instead, she spent the next 30 minutes or so presumably inconsolable in the ladies toilets. The accounts manager offered further 'sympathy' when she did reappear, to which she reacted with some disdain, stressing a desire for people to just treat her normally.

I'd never lost anyone close to me at that point. My grandparents died when I was very young, and I was old enough to have fond memories of them, but not to have a great feeling of loss or grief about them not being around, so I couldn't really relate to what my office chum was going through.

My first interaction with Annie came in the company's archive room. 'Are you lost?' I quipped. 'This is where we put all the files you throw at us.' It was not dissimilar to what I might have said to her the previous week, month or year and I thought little of it. But months later, she thanked me for helping her deal with her grief. I was shocked, thinking I must have come to work drunk and done something I couldn't recall, but no. She cited the throwaway quip by the filing cabinet on her first day back as the most significant help she'd had to pull herself together at the office.

I took away from that experience that grieving people sometimes just want to be treated normally. So would it really help to talk about it to a stranger?

I was going to find out. Cruse Bereavement Care generously agreed to assign a counsellor to me.

Heading to my maiden counselling session, I was nervous. This was the first time post Sam's death that I was actually doing something for myself, by myself. I arrived with plenty of time to spare, and was escorted to a waiting room in a solitary, cold and lonely building that Cruse were using. It was a very sombre setting, and made me relax a little rather than making me feel more uptight.

My counsellor came and fetched me. I wasn't sure what to expect. I guess I was half-expecting a flowery hippy type to meet me and instantly offer me a joss stick. There was no joss stick. Instead, there was an unapologetic sturdy lady with an envelope in her hand.

On sitting down, her first action was not to offer me a tissue, but to offer me the envelope.

'This is what your doctor wrote about you,' she said. 'I'd like you to read it.'

I was a little shocked with it in my hands. 'Shit,' I thought. I really am going to have to be open and honest here. And what the hell is in this letter?

The counsellor paused and let me read the relatively short note from my GP. It detailed the loss I'd just experienced, and the combined stresses of a potential return to work and being the sole parent to a newborn. It also said something like, 'While I don't fear for his immediate health and state of mind, I feel a period of counselling may help prevent a potential downward spiral into considering self-harm and worse.'

WHAT?

I was in no way offended by what the doctor had written. I believed at the time – and still do – that he was excellent with me. But this was the first time that I realised he feared for my health, perhaps not immediately, but that given the wrong set of circumstances he was concerned that I may end up hurting myself.

My counsellor asked if I agreed with the letter, but also said that it was unimportant as she would be forming her own opinion, and any feeling I had, however irrational, was valid, because, well, I was having it.

It was a refreshingly open exchange and properly set the tone and boundaries. She emphasised that she could only help me if I engaged with the process and was completely open and honest with her.

Which I was.

The sessions are still a bit of a haze and I struggle to remember the detail. But I do recall that this is when I rediscovered a limited ability to focus. During our discussions, while I could get distracted and distant, I could also manage to think about things other than Max's next bottle with more clarity. I'd get upset, but didn't feel that I was being poked with an emotional stick to evoke those feelings. In fact, often the counsellor would stop me and ask why I was crying. What emotion was I feeling and why? Was it productive, or a cycle of feeling sorry for myself?

As I've mentioned before, of all the things I felt when I became a widower, I do know an overriding feeling of gratitude was among them. I was grateful for having had the love of Samantha, grateful for the time we'd had together. Grateful for the beautiful boy our relationship had produced. I was reminded of these things during counselling.

The old adage (or should that be cliché?) that someone always has it worse is something I relied on, too. As horrible as it is to be widowed, there is always someone worse off than you. In my case, I had my son who'd lost his mother, someone he'd never get to know. His situation was worse than mine, and that's before we even started looking outside to the rest of the world's many woes. I probably lived next door to people who had suffered worse than me, and that was a powerful thought for me too.

I found myself agreeing a lot with what the counsellor said, which wasn't much. I think it was more her job to let me draw conclusions or get to the answer myself. She helped me a great deal with the process of getting to know myself and what was going to work for me. We agreed that I'd made a good call by not going back to live at our old home. She complimented me on being aware of not tainting my memories, giving me more credit than I'm sure was due.

Because I felt she understood what I was saying, and given that she had no other motive in talking to me, I felt her opinion was unbiased, and that made it easy to talk to her. She would happily disagree with me, whereas family and friends might have chosen to agree with me regardless of their real thoughts.

Our work was centred on me visualising a new future for myself, and Max, and giving up on the life we'd had before with Sam. It was reassuring to think that there were conclusions I was coming to myself, and that this figurative mountain of a woman completely understood. We spoke about true love, and how continuing along the same path of life now would, if anything, be a little disrespectful of the path we'd shared together. We discussed how dwelling on the many ways in which Samantha was missing from all we did would make it difficult for me to mend, and that I could perhaps even grow resentful of her.

I realise now that, during our sessions, the focus on some sort of future, a different future, is something counsellors do with people they are worried may eventually think about taking their own lives. If someone doesn't talk about the future, they use that as an indication for potential self-harm. I guess if I had read the grieving textbooks I'd have known that. But it didn't really matter. At the outset of those meetings, taking my own life had never even entered my mind. To that point, in the darkest of my days, I'd have perhaps thought about wishing to swap places with Sam, for Max to be able to trade me for a life with his mother instead.

But I guess those days weren't actually my darkest.

# 8.
# The only way is not down

My wife loved holidays. I take a great deal of solace in the fact that her eventual end came while she was enjoying one, with the people she was closest to.

Going away was something of an obsession for Samantha. She was a planner, someone who would have the months ahead largely mapped out, and the first things to be inked into our diary were always breaks away from home. As a couple in full-time, well-paid employment, I saw holidays as a luxury that could be justified as easily as they were afforded. What I mean is, uninterrupted time away together was good for our relationship, easing the pain and inconvenience of having to go to work for the vast majority of our time. I always enjoyed a week or two of the phone not ringing and getting completely lost in a book, or seven, on holiday.

That was something we did completely agree on – that while on holiday, the priority was to do, in fact, nothing, and 'nothing' means lounging about reading a novel. I'd have killed for a Kindle back in those days. My airplane luggage allowance would be dominated by books. Having seven, or perhaps twelve for a fortnight away, would not be unusual for me.

This was the mode we would enter on holiday: heads down and read. Hunger was generally the only thing to disturb us.

Samantha loved being away, and whilst we tended to travel to different places each time, I wouldn't say that either of us was particularly travelling to discover the world. The scenery, the people and whatever else we discovered were generally gorgeous secondary benefits to our primary desire to relax and spend time together. We went all over Europe, with Italy becoming an increasingly favourite destination for sun-drenched holidays, and the French Alps being a favourite for our winter excursions.

Sam was determined that having children wasn't going to change her outlook on holidays. We were still going to take overseas breaks. Our opinions differed somewhat here. I personally didn't much see the point in foreign breaks even before children, but she was insistent they were an absolute necessity for us, that our imminent trio must be taking overseas trips together. She went further, to suggest that we should be prepared for, and even actively encourage, our parents to join us on holiday from now on.

I raised several objections. I didn't think that she'd thought the whole thing through. What she was describing as a holiday now was completely unrecognisable from the breaks we'd taken together before. Did she totally understand the changes that taking a child on holiday abroad would entail? Had she never experienced the inescapable irritation of a crying baby on a plane? How about protecting a baby from the sun? And how would all the restrictions on carrying liquids impact on how we fed and watered our child? Wouldn't we need to take a car seat with us? There were any number of hassles I could think of to make foreign travel with an infant sound ridiculous.

While these rational arguments didn't fall on deaf ears, she would cleverly argue against them irrationally, with emotional points. She'd say things like: 'But I want to go away', and 'I reckon our child would love the beach', or 'Think of the memories we will all have.'

Compromise was always going to be the result. When Samantha was pregnant with Max, she was insistent upon a holiday. I thought she would be better putting her feet up at home, or somewhere not very far away, and that I'd have time off work to be with her, but that didn't wash and we ended up on a Mediterranean cruise with Sam's parents. Somehow this had been sold to me as a compromise – as I write this nearly ten years later, I still don't really know how. I think the relaxing nature of being on a large boat, and not having to move anywhere but still getting to see some of the most beautiful coastal spots of Europe, had me agreeing. Plus having her mother with her would mean that they could relax together if Sam's dad and I wanted to go off and explore. Or I could just have agreed on the basis that I'd be spared the relative hell of Samantha moaning during the whole duration of my proposed 'stay-cation'.

In retrospect I had to agree we'd made the right call. We had a fantastic cruise, and it was nothing very strenuous for my pregnant wife. But this didn't stop me arguing the case for not going away again once our child was born.

'I don't much see the point of a foreign holiday until our child is at least ten,' I remember saying.

'I was thinking about ten months old, too,' Sam replied.

She knew full well I'd meant years. There was always humour in these discussions, and I don't recall a time that we would really come close to any sort of fall-out over them. I think it was actually indicative of a very healthy relationship that we could talk about our differing ideas and opinions, but still remain rooted in love, and ultimately accept that sometimes we do things to make the other happy. If the worst thing you ever have to do in your life, or in any relationship, is to go a tad reluctantly on holiday, then count yourself very, very lucky – I certainly did.

That ten-month mark did become something of a watershed for a potential foreign holiday. We'd both invested time in finding out about stages of development for our child, hoping that we'd understand what these would mean when travelling, and ultimately decided that it wouldn't be too much hassle to go once our kid was eating solids, crawling, but not walking. We'd look for short-ish flights that might coincide with possible sleep times, and first of all we'd try a UK stay somewhere, to see how we got on and what equipment we really needed.

Both holidays were booked, the first with Samantha's parents, and the later, foreign one with my own.

If you've been paying attention you'll realise that Samantha never got to go on the second holiday. She died whilst we were on holiday with her parents in a beautiful English cottage.

Samantha dying was horrific, watching her fight for her life, witnessing her parents' pain as well as feeling my own. But certainly the practicalities could have been so, so much worse. If we'd chosen to holiday abroad, in a place unknown to any of us, in a country speaking a different language, where getting home – and getting Samantha back – would not have been a matter of finding someone fit enough to drive a car for a couple of hours … It's a scenario I am grateful to have been spared. I guess it wouldn't have changed anything, but it's some comfort that we weren't any further afield than Somerset.

The thing is, we still had the second holiday booked. The trip abroad that was scheduled to be our first as a very young family.

Sam died on the 2nd of August 2005, officially at some time between two and three in the morning. The holiday was booked for October, nearly Sam's birthday, and coinciding with my sister's planned honeymoon.

Sam had been playing a big part in helping my sister, Emma, to plan her wedding. Armed with a library of recent information she had amassed to plan our own wedding a couple of years previously, she bravely put herself forward to help Emma and her fiancée Ray plan the perfect day. Ray had nicknamed Sam 'the wedding monster', as her mere presence meant he was about to be presented with a decision to make or opinion to offer on invitation types, venues, colours, themes, wedding attire and the like. It was always well meant, though, and even Ray would have agreed how much easier Samantha made things for them.

I'm sure for Emma it felt like she'd lost a sister. They'd become incredibly close in the five or six years they'd known each other, proper friends. It was wonderful for me to see two people I loved so much developing such a strong bond and love for one another. And it now meant we were sharing immense grief and loss together.

Emma and Ray had a big call to make. Would they still carry on with the wedding? Samantha had been such an integral part of the planning, and of course the family. Would it be right to continue without her? They were incredibly considerate of me, almost suggesting it was my decision to make. We discussed it, but I pointed out it really was little to do with me. As sad as it was that Samantha had died, it didn't change the fact that Emma and Ray wanted to declare their love for each other in this way. They decided to get married as planned, not least because they thought the always thoughtful and selfless Samantha would be cussing them if they'd have postponed or cancelled the wedding because of her.

It was a special day of course. Poignant reference was made to the absent 'wedding monster', who was certainly there in spirit for all the celebrations. I managed to get through it – and the speech as best man, too – with a brave face, in the knowledge that I still had my own decision to make.

Should I honour the holiday that Samantha had booked? She'd have so looked forward to it, and like Emma and Ray, I envisaged her being angry with me if I cancelled it. Would I curse myself if I'd not gone? Would I regret going? Which would be worse?

One thing that helped make my decision was that my sister, the person I'd probably become most reliant on after Sam's death, would be out of the country for three weeks on her honeymoon. She'd been brilliant to me, putting herself out at the drop of a hat to spend time with me, giving up whatever else she had planned to be at my side when I wanted someone to talk to or just be with. She protected me from a lot of shit, was a fabulous sounding board, and of all the figurative shoulders I had to cry on, hers was easily the most comfortable.

I was genuinely going to miss Emma. And I worried about how her temporary absence would affect my state of mind. The intensity of my grief was probably at its worse during this time. The immediate shock and numbness had passed, the impact on others was not as overt as it had been, and I'd become terribly lonely. I felt few understood, and many of my friends became increasingly absent, or offered me company in situations I wasn't comfortable with. Emma had always been there for me, but now she was going to be away. I wasn't going to begrudge her a honeymoon of course, but I thought that by being away for a week myself, the three weeks, which felt like a monumental amount of time, would be broken up and pass more quickly.

I also concluded that any regret I might have about *not* going would be much bigger than any regret I would have about going.

So with Emma and Ray married and off to the other side of the world for three weeks, I set off for my own holiday. It was the first time that my son would fly, other than when I'd hold him aloft for his Superbaby impressions, and the first time he'd experience a foreign country. My parents were, as planned, with me. We were actually going to a place they'd been plenty of times before, Los Gigantes in Tenerife. It was a regular holiday destination for my parents in the autumn and winter months, chosen for its warm but not exotic climate at that time of year. And the fact that my parents knew the area reasonably well was also one of the reasons I'd reluctantly agreed to book time away together as a small group. My thinking was that if they at least knew where all the amenities and decent restaurants were, we'd be spared the faff of having to find these places, reducing potential holiday stresses.

The plane journey was actually fairly pleasant. Max was brilliantly behaved and the timings worked out so that it didn't interrupt his routine. I think a few passengers around us were intrigued as to where Max's mother was. It really isn't usual for men to travel alone with babies, not that there is a problem with it, but I don't think that people are used to seeing it. Some ask about it, and of course regret that they did. Some make incorrect assumptions – which are really just masked questions – and others, my favourites, just mind their own business.

I guess this was something I was getting increasingly used to – the dangerous assumptions of strangers and the 'Where is his mother?' question. One thing that really hurt about that was that it was sort of implied, before knowing my situation, that Max's mother must be rubbish not to be around. On the way to a holiday that she'd insisted on, not me, things like that were most painful.

I was so organised on that trip that there were very few things I wasn't in control of on the practical side, but any small change to his routine felt monumental and I would get in a state worrying about them. Changes to his food was one of them. Surfaces was another. It might seem ridiculous, but in the UK almost every home is carpeted, and I started to worry if Max would be able to comfortably crawl on the ceramic tiles typical of Spanish holiday rentals. If he couldn't, when he'd only just got used to crawling, would this holiday put back his development? Also, as he'd started to pull himself to a standing position, would the hard floors prove to be a problem should he fall? Things like that really worried me, and added to my thoughts that I might be making a mistake in coming away.

The plan, the one to stick to on holiday, was that Max's routine would stay the same. He'd eat at the same times, he'd bath at the same time, he'd go to bed at the same time. Obviously there were some adaptations I thought we'd have to make, but we had very well-laid plans for those.

Plans that didn't work.

Max went from being as regular as clockwork at home, to simply refusing to sleep. At home, while I was exhausted from my own lack of sleep and getting up in the night and early with Max, he slept very well. He'd nap at a regular times in the day, and go to bed without much fuss in the evening. Now we were away and he was unsettled. In my fragile and tired state it was quickly becoming very difficult for me.

Drained of confidence, I started to doubt my decision-making and worry about the damage I'd done to my beautiful boy and his routine. Would this ruin all the good work that had been done up to this point? When we got home would I face the same problems?

I missed Samantha desperately. I felt so alone, and so sad. My parents were there and they were trying to help, but by trying to help they were making me feel even more useless, worthless and without purpose. All sorts of horrible things were swirling around in my head. What the hell had I done coming away on holiday with a baby, when I knew there was absolutely no point in it? How had I come to that decision? What other decisions could I be getting wrong? I was so tired, a living zombie, on a holiday from hell.

Persisting with the usual routine on the third evening I bathed Max with a lavender extract shampoo, put him in a fresh baby grow, and took him out for a hillside walk in his pushchair, hopeful he'd drop off. I instructed my parents to follow in about 30 minutes if I'd not come back by then.

Some people don't like Los Gigantes, or Tenerife in general, saying that it is very barren, like the surface of the moon. But I think it can be really pretty at dusk. It was quite windy that night, and the sea was gently crashing – if that's possible – against the steep hills of Los Gigantes. It was the perfect setting to go to sleep. If I'd have been reclined in a stroller, freshly bathed, snug in a new neck-to-toe baby grow, listening to the sea lap the shore, all whilst the sun was coming down over the sea, I'd have been asleep forever.

Max had other ideas. He was wide awake.

I was hungry, exhausted, desperate and missing Sam like never before. I tried talking to her, seeing if she could come up with any ideas, but there were none. I even got the feeling that at this point she'd have been screaming at me that holidaying with a baby was a ridiculous idea.

Max and I were now perched on top of a cliff, watching the sunset, and the swell of the sea was almost directly beneath us. He was perfectly satisfied – it was me in tears. We neared the edge of the cliff, and I looked down at the rocks. It reminded me of scenes from the seaside during my childhood, only I'd never felt the way I did now.

I wanted to be in the water. I wanted to be under the water. At least there I would find peace from my pain. It looked like home.

Then I turned to my boy, and realised he was my home.

I don't know how long we stood there, at what point I realised that this was my new low point, and that we were going no lower. But I did.

Tomorrow was another day, and I was going to treat it as such.

# 9.
# You're very brave

The one thing, or the most positive thing, I discovered about myself while abroad with my son for the first time was that getting out and about is what we needed to be doing.

I think it would be excusable, given the circumstances, if I had spent the majority of my, or our, time in relative isolation. Choosing to stay at home rather than going out. Choosing to bake cakes in our own kitchen rather than join in at a playgroup. Choosing to invite friends over, rather than go and make new ones. But I had discovered that while that would perhaps be understandable, it wouldn't have been doing either of us any good.

There are massive benefits for both parent and child in regularly venturing out to classes and groups. I'm sure there are many parenting experts who can eloquently explain these respective virtues, but for me it was fairly obvious. Of course I was mindful of the social and physical developments my child would make when having to deal with strangers, perhaps other children wanting the same toy or book to play with, as well as combating the different physical challenges a soft play area, swimming pool or ball park might offer. I'd read about and researched some of these benefits, and others are just plainly logical (I won't use the word 'common sense', as I'm unsure sense is, in fact, still common).

It made sense to me that if I was taking my son to visit and engage with groups of unknown children of a similar age, he would get an opportunity to develop friendships, to understand the principle of sharing, as well as get used to being around different people than those known to him. It was also obvious that a lot of these places would have people there with immense experience of working with children, providing fun and proven activities that would not only be enjoyable for my child, but would also be aiding his development, and perhaps providing me with more ideas for games and activities at home.

These are things Sam and I had discussed as young parents, and probably before that. We were both sold on the benefits of parent and toddler groups, play and stay sessions, soft play centres, swimming splash, rhyme time and whatever else there was out there. Samantha spent a good deal of time discovering groups and children's centres around us, as well as finding friends with children who were already visiting similar places.

Sam would also talk about the social aspect for herself. How she'd read about the common feeling of isolation in new mothers, and how getting yourself and your baby to groups of this nature can be of benefit to both mother and child. I listened to those arguments, and agreed with her, but always thought that was a secondary function and that Sam, being the social person she was, would never be isolated in any case.

One facet we hadn't discussed, as I suppose it wouldn't have been relevant, was how just having someplace to go can have an impact on your mood. I'm guessing a sense of purpose is something everyone needs, a purpose that is enough not just to get you up in the morning, but to do it with a smile on your face.

Max was my obvious purpose. As an infant, he needed constant attention. Time for a feed, a bottle, winding, a nappy change, time out of his nappy to kick his legs and let his bottom breathe, a nap, a bath, a change of clothes, his nails clipped, his hair brushed, his face and hands wiped, all leading to getting him off to sleep for the night for a repeat show tomorrow. I'm sure there are functional tasks I've failed to list, and I've made absolutely no reference to the need to think about stimulating him throughout the day with reading, drawing, building, pretending he can fly, or blowing on his belly.

But if you aren't careful this can become an all-consuming cycle of crap, quite literally. Baby care can be a little processional, inevitable, and dare I say it, boring. Minute details can also seem of huge importance, especially when there's little else going on around you. Missing a regular feed time by ten minutes could start to get you agitated, and you'd blame that for you and your child being in a bad mood for the rest of the day.

After that low, low point of our holiday in Los Gigantes, I realised that these little disruptions weren't really the reason I was feeling so down. In fact I needed to be doing more to make us both feel better, to lighten the mood. That's why I decided we would spend the rest of the holiday still sticking to a fairly regimented routine and timetable, but do it around activities that saw us out of the house or holiday apartment, and only back when we needed to be.

In Tenerife I let go of something, I still don't know quite what. Perhaps it was being so very hard on myself for missing any beat of my self-imposed parenting drum. At the time I don't think it was a profound, sudden self-awareness. It was more a case of thinking, 'Stop feeling sorry for yourself, stop worrying about every single thing, and tomorrow, get out of the apartment.'

The second half of that week in the Canaries was very different to the first. It was clear I'd been on a downward spiral for the first few days, partly on a comedown after my sister's wedding, but also because I was putting myself in a situation of achieving nothing other than replicating our home routine abroad, with any deviation feeling like a massive failure. But now I looked for things to do. If we got out in the morning and went down to the pool for an hour, Max would be tired. I worked out he could then nap in the car on the way to somewhere. The first place we ventured out to was called Jungle Park. With its tropical forest setting, winding paths, seemingly uncaged animals and birds of prey show, it was a fantastic day out. Max, myself and my parents all got a great deal out of that day, not only because we enjoyed its attractions and Max's reaction to them, but because it signified and brought about an immense change of mood and spirit.

My parents aren't fools and I am sure they were very aware of my state of mind, perhaps even blaming themselves a little bit for being in on the holiday, and I am sure it was a relief for them to witness the mass improvement in my frame of mind. I'd gone from perhaps the darkest point of mourning Samantha to being able to find at least some joy in life, and while I was still exhausted – probably even more than I had been before – it suddenly felt right to be on holiday.

The ethos of scheduling day trips around Max's routine continued until it was time to go home. Coming back to England was something I looked forward to. There was a certain amount of relief that the holiday was over, and that I'd be more comfortable caring for my boy on home turf, but there was also a sense of satisfaction that it had been the right call after all to go away, and that despite its obvious low, a line had been drawn to which we would never return.

I don't know why, but the holiday had me reflecting on the period since Samantha's death, my immediate adjustment to our new situation, and more specifically, Max's. My son benefited from the wonderful care of his mother for just seven months, but – like I've said to him many times – she had given him the best possible start.

Sam researched a lot, especially things like playgroups. She was going to have a regular routine, meaning Max would have too. One of these groups was a parent and toddler group run at a local church. My mother had some involvement with the parish, so she knew about it, and Samantha decided that she, my mother and Max would become weekly visitors to it. At this particular group, chairs were arranged around the outside wall for the adults, and the toys laid out – informally in differing age ranges and types – in the middle. It was one massive play area for pre-school children to mix and mingle in, and retreat to the perimeter when they needed servicing, or to hide a precious toy they had snaffled from the pile.

It was also the first playgroup that I visited with Max, after Samantha passed away.

I'm not sure why I chose this one. It might have something to do with my mother knowing it, or its proximity to my parents' house. It was also a building familiar to me, as I'd attended a youth club there as a young teenager, as well as occasionally playing badminton in the vast hall.

I think the actual group was called a mother and toddler group. This was one of the lazy assumptions I would regularly encounter. When we were a couple, starting our own family, I don't think I even noticed the group names, and because that's what it was – exclusively a group of mothers and children getting together, albeit with a few grandmothers and childminders in the mix – no one would have raised any objections. But now, in the midst of grief, I was the only man accompanying a child at this group.

Perhaps sensing my intense desire to be an independent carer for my child, my mother did a vanishing act as we arrived at the door. I parked Max's pushchair in the snooker room, and headed off into the main hall to join the group. It was very noisy, yet eerily disconcerting. I guess I wasn't at my most confident, and things as mundane and non-consequential as paying our fee to join today's group seemed huge. Was the woman sat behind the cash tin going to know my situation? Was there going to be a very awkward moment of me explaining that Max had been a regular visitor, but I hadn't yet, and why?

Luckily he was recognised, and I think my mother reappeared to take care of those formalities, and save me from a painful explanation. So all I had to do was choose somewhere to sit.

I think many parents find playgroups intimidating. There are often clear cliques, groups within groups, people who've known each other before, or have been coming for months or years. With that in mind, I chose a seat with the biggest gap to anyone else either side. It was quite near the door for a quick getaway, near the soft mats laid down for the babies and crawlers, and about four plastic seat widths from any other living soul. But it didn't stop people talking, or trying to talk, to me.

It was taking all my energy and focus not to become completely overwhelmed by the situation I was in. I was keeping my head down, trying to mask my reluctance to make absolutely any eye contact, being overly attentive to my ten-month-old boy. If he was going to throw a wobbly, this would have been a very good time to do it. Instead he was happy exploring the things and the people around him, which, if you've ever been in that situation, you know will naturally lead you into smaller interactions and quips with other people – commenting on other people's children, asking how old they are, imploring your own to stop staring.

A quick scan of the room had already established that I was the only man in the building. Or the only adult male. I estimate that between 20 and 40 adults visit that group each week, and I was the only one with dangly bits.

'You are very brave.'

It took me a little while to work out where these words had come from. With my mother off helping with the preparation of drinks and toast for the children's snack time, I was left without my social barrier. But I looked up to discover it was a lady, presumably a mother, sat on her own those four seats down from me.

I managed to afford her a little nod, in the desperate hope that this would be the sum total of my interaction with adults at that day's group meet-up.

'No, you really are brave,' she said, 'My husband wouldn't sit where you are now.'

I tried the nod again, not looking her in the eye, instead casting my gaze in the direction of my boy. I think I even took to the floor myself, so it was my back that faced the lines of seated women. She must have thought I was so rude. But had I tried to talk to her, I know it would only have ended one way – with me in tears – and I'm guessing that would have made her feel bad.

Thing is, just how brave was I being? This was only a playgroup, somewhere Max had been coming for weeks beforehand. I was as uncomfortable as I'd ever been, but I knew we were in the right place, that there was going to have to be a first time for things like this, and however difficult I was going to find them, it shouldn't stop us doing them. Watching my son explore, interacting with me and other kids (yes, I still consider myself a kid, too), was brilliant.

The fact that he was playing happily and not showing any signs of having his memory jogged by being there, and thus pining for his mother, was reassuring, too. I certainly didn't want Max to forget his mother, and if he was able to retain any memory of her living I would encourage him to do so, but I didn't want him to be affected by her sudden absence. I was struck by regular reminders that it should have been Samantha sat where I was, or more likely, at the centre of it all. With every smile I received or witnessed from the boy, there were opposing emotions of sharing his joy, and the pain of feeling I shouldn't be the one enjoying them.

As time went on, our attendance at this group became regular, and – mainly through engaging and interacting with other children – I grew in confidence and increased my engagement level. My chin moved slowly away from my chest and I started to talk to other parents and carers at the group. I got past caring what anyone thought if I became emotional there, or if by sharing our situation, I upset others. Nothing was going to change what had happened, and I didn't want the subject to be taboo, or difficult to discuss around Max. I don't think it would be right to constantly ram down his, or anyone's, throat that his mother had died, but I wanted him to understand that she had, and that everything was going to be okay. Part of this meant I was going to have to make it totally acceptable to talk about the subject.

As it happens, having a man at a playgroup like that that was so unusual that people were always on the hunt for an explanation. It seems it isn't enough for people to make assumptions, like they do when a mother turns up with a child for the first time. There must be something 'up' or odd for a man to be the one providing the childcare. However, as painful as my situation was to explain sometimes, it was very clear-cut, and people didn't need to ask twice for an explanation.

Not that everyone did ask. I guess some weren't overly interested, and others would have learned of my plight on the playgroup grapevine. An 'I'm here because my wife is dead' T-shirt was unnecessary, and I eventually took it as a compliment, and a sign of my behaviour at the group, that people didn't guess it.

Playgroups turned into a great resource for me as a parent. Not only because of what my son would get up to and enjoy while at them, but because I could witness the varying stages of expected development, simply by casting my eye over the children slightly older than my boy. The mothers were also useful, often without realising it. I'd ask them questions, or get into discussions that would reveal their particular answers to parenting conundrums. Sometimes I'd even canvass the expertise of people whose children *weren't* ones I wanted my son to emulate, looking for what to avoid.

In this way, I began to make tentative inroads into the public world of parenting, finding my place and discovering there was even more to this job than I'd previously thought.

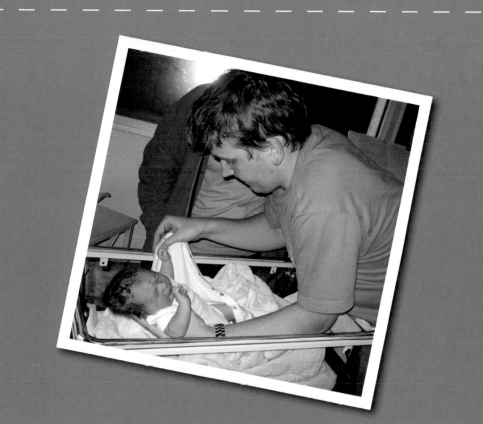

# 10.
# Fighting them off

What do you do when someone around you is suffering with bereavement?

That's a very difficult question to answer specifically. I don't think it would be too bold to say that it's impossible to have an answer that will suit all situations and all people. But I guess that most people's instinct is to try and help in some way.

When Samantha died I was blindsided into a state of shock, struggling to take in what had happened, and what would happen. I found myself in an almost permanent state of bewilderment, overwhelmed and was absorbed in my personal grief, and such were the magnitude of these feelings, it took a while for me to be able to see the situation from anyone else's point of view.

But in the aftermath of someone you love suffering a loss, I can see that there's undoubtedly an impulse that you must do something to help the situation. It was something I'd felt the very time I first met Sam, and her grandfather was dying. I didn't know her. I'll never be sure that baring my bruised bottom to her was the right way to go, but the basic compulsion to come to the aid of someone in grief was natural.

Now the people that knew us both were feeling the same need to help. Though hopefully none of them would think it appropriate to bare their butts for me.

In our situation, Max's grandparents had their own grief to deal with, as well as the sorrow they felt for their first and only grandchild, and for me. For Sam's mum and dad, I think there was also an almost instant worry about the impact their daughter's death would have on their long-term relationship with their grandson. They were having to consider the possibility of me finding it easier to limit their involvement, or even cut them out of my and Max's life altogether. They had no way of knowing what was going on in my head, but as muddled as I was, it was never part of my thought process to do anything of the sort. These were Max's loving, brilliant grandparents, and the tragic loss of his mother did nothing to change that. If anything, they now had the added responsibility of helping him to learn more about his mother's life. As well as I knew and loved

Samantha, I didn't know everything about her and her childhood. If Max were ever to become curious about it in the future, it would be them I'd suggest he ask.

But grandparent involvement was an issue. It was before Samantha died, and now it was going to be again.

We had the somewhat enviable problem of having two incredibly keen sets of nans and grandpas wanting to be involved and around their first grandchild as much as was possible. It's not a situation I think it fair to complain about too much, as lots of new families aren't anywhere near as lucky as we were, and while we always appreciated the help, and the freedom it was going to allow us, it was important for us to have our own time too. As a new family unit, it became clear to us that we needed to set precedents for quality time on our own. Our family weren't supposed to feel left out – more just appreciative that we wanted time together as an uninterrupted unit, and that it meant our doors wouldn't always be open. That might sound harsh and selfish, but as first-time parents we were sure we were doing the right thing, and that everyone understood that.

For me, it had always been important to establish myself as Max's parent. You might say that it's daft to feel that way, and that as the fertiliser of his egg I'd probably already done that, but there was an inner need for me to prove myself a competent carer and not always feel like I was playing second fiddle behind all the female family members in his life.

For many men I think there's a tendency to feel a bit like a 'back up parent', especially when the kids are babies. As we are typically off at work and not at home with the child, this can even sometimes extend to a feeling of falling behind secondary care-givers, like grandmas, in importance. I didn't want to feel that way.

Now, as his only living parent, this was going to be even more important to me, but it wasn't as if I hadn't fought hard to establish myself already, I started that fight only hours after his birth, when it was time to put Max in his cot, and in clothes, for the first time. By this time my mother and sister were our two permitted visitors. And instead of hearing and responding to my question 'How do I put this on?' with instructions or tips, my mum tried to take over.

It's a common instinct to want to complete tasks yourself rather than take more time explaining to someone else how to do it. I've done it myself. But equally this was one of those times for establishing that I was after guidance, rather than substitution. It wasn't the old trick of pretending not to know how to do something so someone else will take over – I'm a dab hand at looking all confused at a vacuum cleaner – but genuine naivety. That first time, I literally had to fight my mother off so I could dress Max myself.

And now, again, it was perhaps time to re-establish myself. I'd have been a more than able secondary carer, 'the back-up parent', but now it was time for me to step up.

Moving back in with my parents perhaps brought people to the natural conclusion that my mother would be heavily involved in Max's care, with some even expecting me to play the supporting role once again, as I'd done with Sam. I'm not for one minute rubbishing my mother's parenting skills (insert 'She raised me and I turned out OK' gag), but I didn't think that was the right way to go.

There were lots of things, despite some contrary opinions, that kept bringing me to the conclusion that as Max's sole parent I should act as such, and use my army of very willing helpers when it suited both Max and I, rather than as a matter of course.

For myself, there was the desire to establish my identity as Max's dad, my desperation for a purpose. Before, as the breadwinner, I had my place and functions in our family unit, and I was very happy with them, albeit at times a little jealous of my wife's time with our boy. But now the role I'd played before wasn't going to suit me, or us. I couldn't see the point in going out to earn more money than we really needed. I wanted to focus on the things that were really important to me, rather than providing cash for material luxuries we'd come to take for granted before.

For Max, I wanted to generate and reinforce feelings of love, to make him feel wanted. I feared that by losing his mother, any instance of me not being around might be heightened, and even possibly interpreted as abandonment. I don't know how rational or likely that would have been for a baby to feel, but the reality was, and always will be, that he is massively loved, and was brought into the world because of it. I didn't want him to ever feel less than loved, and certainly never like an inconvenience to anyone.

I also wanted consistency in his life, for him to have clear boundaries and routines. Having his care split between lots of people and places introduced the possibility of inconsistency. But at the same time I recognised that I mustn't smother him, become too dependent on him, or exhaust and burn myself out trying to juggle absolutely everything without help.

It also just felt right to be with him full time. Being around Max has always brought me calmness, and a fantastically spiritual reward, even with the most simple of things. With him, no matter where we are, I always feel at home.

So as well-meaning as the grandmas were, as much as their offers to help were valued and welcome, I think I was somewhat forcing them to repress their urges to help. They could actually help me by letting me take the absolute undisputed lead with Max's care.

I understood they also had their own needs to satisfy in terms of finding things to do in the wake of Samantha's death. For Samantha's mother, she'd lost a daughter to whom she'd been very close. They were like best friends as well as mother and daughter. Samantha's absence was not only very painful, it left a practical void as well as a psychological one. I was mindful to be respectful of that, but didn't want any decisions I made to be based solely on the needs of Sam's grieving mother.

I devised an informal but regular weekly routine that meant Max and I would spend one day a week with Sam's mum. Often we were joined by one of Sam's friends and her son on our adventures. This is the sort of day that would probably have happened and found its place in Max's schedule if things had all remained equal – except now these lovely women and children were stuck with me for company rather than blessed with Sam's.

There was a similar day scheduled with my own mother, and actually, my dad. As they were both retired, we'd generally spend a Wednesday morning with my mum at the church playgroup, and the afternoon on a more ad-hoc basis with my dad. We'd go for a stroll to the local park, or to soft play centres if we needed to be indoors.

This left Max and I some days on our own, or that I'd spend with other friends, plus the weekends. I decided that it would also make sense to have a chance to recharge my batteries, to eventually pursue other interests and perform mundane tasks such as shopping and cleaning without worrying about Max's entertainment. So he spent the majority of his Mondays with my parents, and the majority of his Saturdays with Sam's. I'd designate one as a domestic day, sorting out all my chores and tasks, and the other would be for me to relax and find things to do for myself.

There were breaks from this normal routine when other things cropped up, or Max and I went off visiting friends further afield, but it was generally how our weeks played out. It certainly suited us, but I feel some guilt at times for the effect it was perhaps having on those close to us, particularly the grandmas. I hope I am right in thinking that they all knew I was limiting their involvement out of good intentions, and certainly not out of spite. Their contributions were of immense value, and I knew I could call on them if I needed them any more than was normal, but equally I felt the need to be with Max on my own and unaided.

It was a philosophy I stand by and believe worked. There's nothing like being thrown in at the deep end, and I felt like not having figurative arm bands certainly helped me learn to swim.

Max also responded well to it. Our bond was growing closer by the day, the hour, the minute. I loved the fact that he was comfortable depending on me – and he probably still has no idea just how much I was dependent on him.

# 11.
# Facing facts and sharing grief

There's no escaping death. It will come to us all.

How's that for a pointing-out-the-obvious cheery chapter opening?

In the first twenty-seven years of my life, I'd done well to avoid it. And I don't mean managing to survive to that point myself. More that I'd lived in a little bubble that was un-pierced by the huge dagger of loss.

I think, like many people, I thought I knew what loss was, or how it might feel before I'd even experienced it myself. You watch friends go through things – losing parents, siblings, grandparents, even children – and think you know what they are going through, how they feel, and how it affects them. But it really is a case of living in ignorant bliss.

People suffering loss *emit* grief. You can feel, and see, their pain, sometimes even noticing a physical difference in them. They may lose weight. They may change colour, looking all washed out, shadows of their former selves. But you still have no idea what is going on in their heads.

Previously the biggest losses I'd suffered were that of family pets. Not exactly comparable, but it's all I had. Those were the only feelings of grief I could call on. I'm not entirely sure how old I was, perhaps eight or nine, but I have a distinct and rather embarrassing memory of inconsolably weeping over the loss of our family cat. I recall my little sister and I being either side of the cat's chair, heads touching the seat it used to sleep on, and both of us sobbing. And not on a single occasion, but day after day, from when we got home from school until bedtime.

The others, involving actual human beings, were memories of my grandparents' deaths. But these were from when I was even younger, and weren't particularly vivid. My mother's parents, who were significantly older than my other set of grandparents, died when I was not much older than a toddler. My granddad died first. I don't really recall it at all, though my memories of him are fond. I paint a picture of a lovely older man, who used to buy and sneak me sweets. It was slightly different with my nan. I still have the fond memories, again sugar-based. She used to let me drink tea with as many sugars in as I fancied. I remember her being left on her own, I remember her going to a nursing home as her health deteriorated, I remember her coming home to be looked after there, and I vividly remember my mother answering our door to my nan's nurse who'd brought us the news of her passing. But still I don't remember getting massively upset, or a prolonged period of sadness.

Perhaps my parents had protected me from it at the time, and should I now be doing the same for my son? It's natural, I suppose, for parents to shelter their offspring from the woes of the world, or their particular little worlds, but there are just some things it isn't possible or practical to shield them from. For me, the overriding memories of those lost grandparents are positive, and while there's an element of sadness, I think this is more out of the sorrow I feel for my mother losing her parents before her children had grown up, rather than my own feelings of loss. If my parents helped manage that situation for me, then I am grateful to them too. But how was I going to approach doing the very same for my son? Where would I begin? He's lost his mum, it's huge, and how am I – a man really only experiencing grief for the first time now – going to be able to help him?

I feared at first that Max would show signs of missing his mother. I envisaged all-too-painful moments of him helplessly crying, crying for his mother, the one person I couldn't provide for him.

For parents, there's an instant love for newborn children. There certainly was for us, and I think we spent the first few days, weeks and months looking for signs of it being reciprocated. Babies are comforted by many things – by being cleaned and bathed, by having their hunger or thirst satisfied or by being burped out of discomfort. They also like familiarity and being held. I can remember the midwives warning us of the pitfalls of picking up a baby from their crib, cot or basket. Allowing a child to fall to sleep on you would mean that they may not want to go to sleep anywhere else.

I've also seen babies being passed to people who they've either settled with instantly – 'He likes you, you have the touch' – while others have set their waterworks off – 'Oh, I think he wants his mom' or 'He doesn't like people who wear glasses.' I'm not sure how much of that is fact, and if a baby can really sense who they are with, but after months of willing our son to demonstrate a desire to be in our company, to love us back, I was now praying for the exact opposite.

Well, not quite the opposite. I wasn't wishing him not to love me or his mum, but I was hoping he wouldn't notice she wasn't around.

I certainly didn't want him to forget her – I never will – but just couldn't handle the thought of him forever pining for a person who couldn't be there.

We'd discussed beforehand what sort of parents we wanted to be, or how we thought we would operate as a family, and quickly came to the same hopes and aspirations. We knew parenthood would change us, but we were also determined that all these changes would be positive and we wouldn't let it consume us totally.

Any child, or children eventually, was going to enhance our lives, but there was still a level of independence we would crave, away from our responsibilities as parents. We would have time for ourselves as a couple, and we would have time for doing our own thing too. This would mean both of us being comfortable left looking after the children, and for our children to be comfortable in the care of others.

It's important to get the balance of that right, and everyone struggles for the perfect mix of being there for your children unconditionally, but also being able to take time away from each other and enjoy our own things.

So our plans and Max's interactions with others meant that he was what people would deem a social baby. He was happy to be passed around a room – not that he had much choice, such was the desire of those close to us to hold him. But still, given that his mother had been his primary care-giver, I anticipated there would be a reaction to her now being absent from his life.

It never came. What I write here is a lot of guesswork, like so much of parenting is for me, but I think it's because I held on to him a lot in the first few days after her death. Even when I was taking him to bed with me for my own comfort, part of me needed to know he felt close and comfortable to me, his one remaining parent. And Max didn't show any physical signs of missing his mother. He took his food and bottles as normal, kept to very similar sleep patterns, and cried like he'd always done for a feed, a clean or a burp.

Which meant I was in charge of someone oblivious to their loss. While it had its benefits, I was already fearful of his day of realisation, or the day I'd have to share the news with him that his mother was dead. But there was no hiding the fact, and as hard as it was, I took the decision that I must be open with that information, and as early as was possible. I didn't want the subject of Max's mother to become taboo.

It started with two kisses at bedtime, one from me, and the other from his late mother. As a baby, he couldn't know why he was getting two kisses at night, but I started to say who they were from in the hope that this was the gentlest way of starting to share this impossibly difficult news with him. Of course, it wasn't always easy to do, and some days I just knew it was going to upset me to give him the double kiss, but I stuck to it. It was something he came to expect; he wasn't satisfied at bedtime without both kisses.

Other children were actually key to figuring out how to break the news to Max as his understanding grew. Unlike adults, children generally do ask the questions they have in their heads. While lots of adults, particularly mums at playgroups, may *want* to ask a man with a baby where the mother is, it was the children who generally did so. 'Where's Max's mum?' they'd ask.

I don't recall exactly the first time it happened, but I remember being a little panicked. What was I going to do? Lie? Give it to them straight? Or perhaps try to change the subject? I didn't want to be the big bad man upsetting all the children, but then again, I didn't really want to lie to them either.

'She died,' I said, immediately fearful of having a crying child on my hands, and shortly after that an angry parent. But they'd just listen to what

I'd said, and accept it and move on. Occasionally they'd say something like 'My granny died, too,' or 'If she's in heaven, do you think she could look after our hamster?' They were often painfully cute, but it helped me that they were inquisitive. It gave me an insight into how my own child may react in the future, and also into what he could expect to get quizzed about by his peers.

At times, children were a bit flummoxed by me telling them that Max's mother had died. I think these were perhaps kids completely unfamiliar with death (almost like my 27-year-old self). They'd want more of an explanation. It is not easy to explain to a child, a stranger's child particularly, the concept of dying. I didn't want to strike fear into their innocent hearts, and I tried to be as gentle as I could with the subject.

I think kids generally struggled with the concept of where people actually are – where being dead physically puts someone. I remember reading that it takes a while for a child to realise that just because someone had left the room, or their sight, doesn't mean they have ceased to exist. With this, it was the opposite. And I started to get very spiritual with my answers.

'She's in our hearts and minds,' I'd say.

It was simultaneously heartbreaking and heart-warming to have my son point to his heart and head when people asked him where his mother was. It was in no way meant as a tactic to 'milk' the situation, or encourage others to feel sorry for him. I actually craved the opposite. I wanted us to being treated like anyone else. I didn't want parents and other children feeling sorry for us, or Max, making concessions for him. I just wanted our normal to be accepted. I wanted Max to be comfortable bringing up the subject, and never be afraid of approaching me, or anyone else for that matter, about it.

There would be times when I would be completely consumed by emotions and grief, and break down in tears. These moments could sometimes be anticipated, and at other times would be unexpected, coming quick as a bolt of lightning on a clear day.

I was at a playgroup about six months after Sam died. Surrounded by children, other parents, childminders, grandparents and group organisers. It was one of my bad days and eventually I found myself overwhelmed, crying. It wasn't as if many of those around me had not seen me emotional before, but I'd say it was sparingly enough for them to be surprised. One of the group's organisers leapt to her feet and tried to take my child away from me. I'm sure her intention was to help, to perhaps free me up so I could go and seek comfort from my own mother, who was with us at the group. But I wouldn't let him go. This was interpreted as me being defensive, and perhaps I was a little. They thought I was trying to physically protest my ability to look after my child, regardless of my emotional state.

There was probably a little bit of truth in those assumptions, but there was something more logical in my actions, too. Rather than protect my son from my grief, I wanted to share it with him, or allow him to share it with me. He could remain oblivious to it as far as I was concerned. I wasn't trying to upset him. But I did want him to know and feel that I was accessible to him at any point in his life, and regardless of my state of mind. If every time I was caught crying, Max would automatically be taken away, I feared he would think that it was him who was upsetting me.

I had some difficulty in putting this view across convincingly. But it was genuinely how I felt. Perhaps it is an instinct to shelter kids from sorrow, but my instinct was, when it seemed right, to share.

I hope I was right about that.

# 12.
# Maternal, smaternal

During my adolescence, as I achieved a semblance of maturity, I'm not sure what my thoughts on becoming a dad were. Coming from a picture-perfect family – two opposite sex parents, bearing one boy (first, obviously) and one girl – I guess I was programmed, to some extent, to attempt to continue production of the same.

In my family, we all played the roles you might have expected us to. My mother stayed at home until my sister and I were old enough for her to return to work, while my dad was the breadwinner, and the sports and clubs chaperone at the weekend. I played the role of the big brother by generally being horrible to my younger sibling, getting away with what I could, and blaming anything else I couldn't on her. She played the little sister part pretty well, too.

This was my normal and something I, perhaps unconsciously, tried to recreate for myself in adulthood. So I guess I always thought I'd become a dad. I just never thought I'd actually need to think about becoming a mum too.

Before I met Samantha, I was more concerned with when my next drinking session was going to be, which team I was playing in at the weekend, or if there was something more interesting on offer than sport. Meeting Sam changed that. Not immediately, but over a period of time, I grew up a bit and gained much more satisfaction from real things, rather than drunken nights out with strangers, and my thoughts would turn to the future, which I hoped would include this gorgeous and brilliant woman who had already changed my life so much for the better.

We'd speak about our futures, and that we both saw each other in them. We were in love, and planning in relatively vague yet common terms, how we wanted our lives to pan out. There was talk of where we wanted to live, in what sort of property, and how that may change over time, especially as we started a family. It was basically a given that we would have children (a potential deal breaker for lots of couples). Sam made it clear she wanted to be a mom, how many children she wanted. I was more of the 'yeah, I'll have kids' attitude. The way I saw it, yes, being a dad felt inevitable for me, and definitely in a good way, but it was something I'd worry about when I got to be one. Samantha was much more aware of what parenthood would entail and what 'type' of mother she wanted to be.

When we got married, we were both in our late twenties, Sam later than me by a couple of years. When we talked about our expectations for married life together, we discussed more specifically our ideas for timing of children, or when we might be attempting to get pregnant. Sam was keen to try early in our married life, and I wanted us to wait a little while. My idea was for us to enjoy an uninterrupted period of married life, and make the best use of our relative affluence to go on those trips she loved, which might become more difficult with the introduction of little ones.

I'd like to say that we compromised, but really I just put across such a good case that Sam ended up agreeing with me. Our attempts at insemination were scheduled for a year after our wedding. Yet when Sam did fall pregnant, I'd still not really thought much more about the practicalities of being a father, the impact of the responsibility, or how it may change me, and us, as a family. And I didn't have much time to think about it then either, because Sam miscarried at around seven weeks.

We were a little surprised that Samantha had even got pregnant. Yes, we knew how babies get made, but the timing of Sam's periods, coupled with us only firing 'live rounds' very recently, meant we thought it would at least be the next cycle before she was with child, at the very earliest. That we got wrong, and an unscheduled bleed took us from a phone call to the NHS to being sat in front of an obstetrician telling us Sam was pregnant but losing the child, all within 24 hours.

Waiting for my wife's body to complete its rejection of this baby was hell. Life carried on as normal. I remember that we even went out for a meal to celebrate a significant family birthday, but we were just waiting for the terrible inevitable. It duly came, one very sad and sombre night. Sam and I lost our first attempt at a child.

I'd not been close to anyone who'd suffered a miscarriage. None of my friends or family had gone through the same, but I'd always been somewhat dismissive of the impact such an event can have, especially so very early on in a pregnancy. I mean, in the stages of development an embryo doesn't exactly look human, so how could anyone attach human connections and emotions to the loss of one?

Well, I learnt the hard way – it's easy.

What we went through together was an experience I wouldn't want to repeat or wish upon anyone else, but it certainly brought us even closer together, and for me, brought what being dad might feel like into sharp focus. It was at that point that I knew I was ready to be a father.

My response to the miscarriage, and my automatic reaction to support Samantha, all made me feel that I clearly, almost instinctively, had wanted to be a dad, and perhaps was better equipped to deal with fatherhood than I'd expected to be before.

We took our time to deal with the miscarriage, processing what had happened, talking to the health professionals about the right time emotionally and physically to start trying again for a child, discussing the statistics, possible reasons for what had happened and the likelihood of a recurrence, before we embarked once more on our attempt to be parents. Again we were very lucky, and after only a cycle or two once we'd started trying again, Samantha was pregnant. She suffered from some bleeding again early on, and the seriously concerned button (panic is not something I recommend) was pressed. But our alarm was short-lived and Sam's pregnancy went rather smoothly overall.

Not that at any time I was relaxed about it. I may have appeared to be from the outside, and I certainly convinced Sam that all was okay, especially when she needed it, but inside I was a desperately nervous clock on a 40-week countdown. At no time did I really look forward to the birth of our first child – I didn't want to get too far ahead of myself. Like the well-trodden sporting clichés, I took each day as it came. It was a game of three trimesters and the boy done good.

I became a dad.

Not a mum.

When Sam died, I was absolutely convinced I could look after Max. But as a dad, one completely able and willing to fulfil all the practical tasks associated with raising a child, wouldn't there also be things I just couldn't do or would forget to consider?

Phrases like 'Only a mum would know' and 'Mum knows best' would start to be less like charming anecdotal small talk and more like devilish taunts that would convince me of a secret underground knowledge I was never going to be part of, and thus that my son would miss out on. Would the lack of a mother, and the impact of a man raising a child alone, mean that my child would be different? Would he be growing up emotionally stunted? What is it that mums provide that dads just can't?

I was convinced there must be some things that don't come naturally to a man. How could we possibly have a 'maternal instinct', the very definition of which would need us to be mothers?

What was I bound to be missing?

It was a question that would circle and circle in my head, driving me a little mad at times, and perhaps eroding my parenting confidence. So I endeavoured to find out what 'it' was that I was missing. No one was going to tell me, partly because I didn't think people knew what it was anyway, and also because not many people fancy telling a recently bereaved parent what they are getting wrong.

My quest to pinpoint 'mother's intuition' was a very practical exercise. I didn't really have the appetite – or time – to be delving through books and formal research for answers. Instead, I went looking for physical evidence and conducted my own analysis by talking to people and observing behaviour.

As an active dad, willing to throw himself into any activity I thought my child might enjoy, there were plenty of opportunities to talk to mums, grandmas and female carers.

There was nothing sinister in what I was doing, and I'm sure it is what a lot of mothers do with one another, too, watching to see how people react to a child's behaviour and how effective their decisions are. I found it especially useful for predicting the next stage or problem my son would present me with, because in groups with children of varying ages, you can see the differences in the children, both physically and in behaviour. If you have a baby who's sitting up, you can watch those that are crawling, who in turn are watching those wrestling themselves to their feet, to those taking their first steps, to those running around, to those riding the balance bikes. Yeah, man, kids grow up fast, and in village halls and community centres all over the world, you can see every developmental stage in its respective glory.

I wasn't sure what I expected to find that I might be missing by default, but I thought I knew what sort of field it would be in. I was expecting the areas I'd be weaker in were going to be the emotional side, the nurturing part of being a parent. I knew, and was comfortable with, all the practicalities of rearing a child, getting them well fed, clothed, clean and in the right place on time, but it was perhaps more how they behaved and interacted with others once they'd got there that I'd fall down on.

I already felt that child discipline was not gender specific. As a child I was comfortable in the knowledge that both mums and dads dished out varying degrees of 'towing the party line'. There are many children brought to book with a 'Wait until your dad gets home', and equally there are many who are used to wrapping their dads around their little fingers, while their mothers deal out the discipline.

But social skills, and the caring side, seemed always to be dominated by mothers. I couldn't really ever recall anyone saying that their dad was better at dealing with them when they were upset, or discussing a delicate matter, or worse, their feelings. And it was, or is, oh-too-common to hear, 'You'll have to ask your mum about that.'

Thing is, Max didn't have one to ask. And I was desperately trying to avoid a scenario of not being able to help him with things men are not expected to be good at.

But what were these things? And what impact would my behaviour now, my interaction and reaction to Max, have on his future development?

I was getting a lot of great information and advice, even if people didn't realise they were giving it to me, but I still had this nagging, persistent worry that there were things I was missing. You know when you are looking for your keys all day and they were in your pocket all along, or when you can't find your glasses, only to realise you've been wearing them for the last hour? It was that sort of feeling.

What I did notice was that some mothers find it difficult to be rational, and do let the worry of how others perceive them influence their judgement. I'd be lying if I said I didn't care what others thought of me, certainly me as a parent, but I think I am pretty good at not letting that be a significant factor in my decision-making. Is that because I'm a man? Or is that because I am just me?

I've always found it easy to be compassionate toward my child, but at the same time I think there is a level of protection that then becomes counterproductive and actually harmful for a kid. I use my logic, probably too much, but not at all in isolation. I wouldn't discount the way something makes you feel as nonsense, and make decisions purely on practical grounds, but I like to believe I make a good balanced call, and that, it appears, I may find easier than some mothers.

I'd hear things like 'I knew it was the wrong thing to do, but she/he was upset,' and what I would think was, 'So you've taught them that they get what they want by being upset?'

Balance, was my conclusion. It is all about balance, and putting your children first. And I don't think it's a maternal instinct, as not all mothers do it. They say they do, and you have to be careful with that one, because why would you ever tell someone the children come first, if not to let people know how selfless you are? 'I don't like to go on about it, but have I told you about my charity work?' That sort of thing.

Perhaps I'm being harsh, and I appreciate that a lot of time parents do it without realising. I'm sure I have.

But I guess I learned that just because you're a woman, and a mum, it doesn't automatically make you a good one.

My quest didn't uncover anything I'd not considered. And thus my parenting confidence grew. It felt right what I was doing, and I felt I was making a reasonable fist of it. I'm compassionate, incredibly comfortable being affectionate to my child, and conversely feel like I don't take any nonsense.

And I do it all without the aid of a vagina.

Although I've been likened to one on occasion.

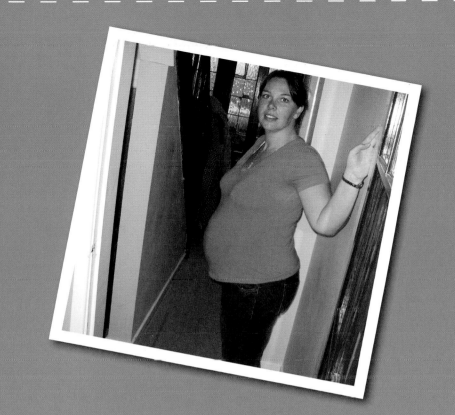

# 13.
# Where's your lovely wife?

There are plenty of social situations that are horrible when you are grieving. Probably most of them. Meeting people for the first time, who have no idea of your recent history. The fear they may ask you a question that would force you to explain it, and possibly upset both of you in the process.

It happened to me a lot. Of course it would. As I've already mentioned, a man with a baby is still uncommon enough for a lot of people's first thought and question to be, 'Where is your baby's mother?' Sometimes the questions are a little sneakier, but ultimately they satisfy the same inquisitive suspicion. 'Does your wife work full-time?' or 'Do you enjoy being the one bringing your baby to the group?' are examples of stealthy snooping.

Some folks may not be confident enough to ask at all. They just become 'all ears' when sitting close to people who are.

Answering questions like that was difficult. I would slump even before taking them on. There isn't really a default answer that works for everyone and every situation. If I was feeling a little more together, it might change the answer I'd go for. At other times I'd be desperately sad, and being cornered into an explanation would make things worse.

It's very difficult to eloquently explain that a baby's mother died when he was just seven months old. It's not an event you can easily downplay or be nonchalant about. That sort of stuff has impact, no matter how you say it. Even if you mumble it. Believe me, I tried it, and many other methods.

That was the other problem. You may be concerning yourself with how explaining your loss will make you feel, but there's having to deal with the reaction from the person asking.

'I'm so sorry, I shouldn't have asked,' watery-eyed mothers would say.

But of course they should. I was grateful to them in way. When my situation was out in the open, it became much easier to deal with in the subsequent weeks, in encounters with the same groups of people. Once I knew that they knew, and they knew that I knew they knew, conversation was easier than it was before. And I found, in a lot of situations, people became more comfortable sharing things with me.

By being adventurous with my son, finding new places and new people to encounter almost daily, situations like this were never far away. And there were the even more awkward times of meeting people from my past, those I knew, but not very well, or those I just hadn't seen for a long time, both groups ignorant of the fact that my wife had died.

The question 'How are you?' is a formidable challenge when you are widower. It takes a lot of energy to repress the urge to say, 'How do think I am?'

There were several memorable occasions when I felt more than awkward. When visiting a cricket club I'd played for in the past, I was walking my boy around the outfield as a game was going on, only to be heckled for not playing anymore. 'Your missus got you under her thumb, has she?' was shouted, to raucous laughter.

Another time, when I answered my parents' front door to one of my dad's old bosses, he was surprised to see me there in the middle of a weekday. 'You've had a baby, haven't you?' he said. 'How are you all doing?'

But what could I do? These were really unavoidable situations, occurrences I knew that, though painful, were ultimately good for me, and much better than being so withdrawn I didn't take the risk of encountering uncomfortable scenarios.

But that's what a lot of social situations became – uncomfortable. I think when you're part of a couple you take certain things for granted, and don't really have any appreciation of the benefits that being a duo bring. Like when you're at a party together, regardless of how many people you know, but especially if that number is low, you have a go-to partner, someone to spend time with, or a base to return to when you've had enough of mingling. It's a practical thing, but it's also something that I drew great enjoyment and comfort from. There might be something you aren't overly looking forward to going to, but with a person you love at your side, you can take things like that in your stride, and actually end up enjoying things you perhaps originally feared.

When you lose that special person, and lose them by any means, the social support crutch you had is gone, and you have to find your place at things like weddings, birthday parties and christenings all on your own. Even meals out with friends can become awkward, especially if you are the only one there without a partner. For anyone, situations like that can be difficult, and ones you try to avoid. But when you've had your confidence sapped by the bereavement monkeys, they become very intimidating, or certainly did for me.

I didn't become reclusive, though, and I knew that it was good for me to spend time away from caring for Max. I tried to keep up with friends, and to still have a social life of my own. It would have been easy for me to become all about my son, living my life vicariously through a baby, but I'd judged that to be unhealthy, and while I did use him as an excuse not to do things on occasion, I was mindful of the benefits of getting out and about solo.

Still, I was torn over justifying time for myself. I'd feel guilty for leaving my son in the care of others, for the sole purpose of entertaining myself with friends. It was ridiculous really. I was generally leaving my boy in the care of grandparents, who were desperate to be spending time with their first grandchild, and only too willing to take Max to the same places I would and further. They were people I wanted him to have brilliant relationships and contact with. But there was still a little paranoia on my part that my son might feel a sense of abandonment. I didn't want my boy to associate me with regularly being absent – sure, time apart is healthy, but not so much that it would feel like like I was getting away from him at every whiff of an opportunity.

My friends and family would say I was being ridiculous at times, and call me out on how I'd generally claim to be guided by rational and logical thinking. And I don't really know how this feeling manifested itself. I did draw comparisons with how, if I was a woman, I may not have been encouraged so much to spend time away from my child, how single mothers out enjoying themselves may not always get a positive reaction from those around them. Were people secretly thinking the same unfair things about me? I wasn't too paranoid about that, but I did always look for greater justification for outings than simply because I thought something would be fun. Events had to have a little importance – like I couldn't really miss a friend's wedding or an important birthday, but drinks or meals for the sake of it generally got a 'Thanks, but no thanks' from me.

I have to be grateful for having wonderful friends and family. Not only were there plenty of people continuing to invite me to things, despite me not exactly being a barrel of laughs, there were a good few who were appreciative of my circumstances and willing to accompany me, so I didn't feel so completely bereft at social functions.

My sister in particular was awesome. We'd always mixed in similar circles, and our relationship was the envy of lots of other siblings we knew, who didn't enjoy quite the same relationship. She's a very popular soul, Emma, and her time is always sought after, but she made me feel like she wanted to be around me, and would have a supportive eye on me when we were out together. She'd be my unofficial partner at social gatherings, or more likely I'd be the gooseberry to Emma and her husband. It certainly lessened the blow of being at things completely on my own, and while I respected the fact that these people needed time for themselves as a couple, it felt reassuring not to really go anywhere without them.

But that didn't completely eradicate the awkward moments. I'm sure they bore the brunt of a good few, explaining my situation to the inquisitive, but the stray enquiry broke through their informal social barricade.

'Where is your lovely wife?' I was asked, by a friend of a friend at a London wedding. It was one of those people who would be borderline for knowing stuff about my circumstances, but her question clearly demonstrated which side of that line she was on.

'Erm, she died,' I managed.

'Oh. The happy couple mentioned that one of their friends had died, I didn't realise that was Sam.'

'No shit,' I replied.

And despite being surrounded by people in a very intimate wedding venue, I had a feeling of detachment from the conversation. Was it really happening? And why could nobody else hear it, and save me the pain?

That moment was bizarre enough, but what followed that day was even stranger. This girl was actually someone Samantha had playfully teased me about in the past. We had a few weekends in London when this girl and her boyfriend had also been part of our weekend gang. We'd got on really well, and I made the mistake of saying how nice I thought she was. This was enough for my mischievous wife to periodically tease me at the infrequent times she came up in conversation, or was referenced by mutual friends –all very good-natured, the kind of teasing you actually like.

But I think Sam would have been shocked by her behaviour. By the end of the wedding, this girl had become a little fixated with me, and had made more than one of what I thought were incredibly inappropriate passes at me. I was not renowned for being a great reader of the opposite sex, Samantha being a very good case in point, but this now-single girl was being ridiculously clear and forthright.

I didn't know how to react. Part of me was angry, some of me bemused, a lot of me wanted Sam to be there. And a tiny little bit of me wanted to tell her, 'Ha, look, she likes me too.'

I sought out my sister and she didn't believe me at first. It was only a few months after Sam had died, and given the earlier foot-in-mouth situation, and how nice this girl had come across in the past, she was sure I was getting it completely wrong. But after shadowing me closely for the next few minutes, Emma also was in no doubts that I was being romantically pursued.

With my sister's help I managed to avoid any further social discomfort, and we decided there was no need to make a big deal of it, laughingly concluding that no one should be chastised for noticing my immense desirability. Except Emma wasn't really laughing, well, not with me anyway.

This woman's approach had caught me by surprise and shocked me a little, mostly as I felt it was so soon after becoming a widower, and a little because I wondered why anyone in their right mind would make a move on me, a single dad amongst a sea of much more eligible bachelors?

As much as it was irrelevant, and not something I wanted to happen, was my situation going to make me more attractive to women?

My new status – not necessarily that of widower, but of outwardly confident and competent single dad, a man completely comfortable looking after his child, and himself for that matter – was it going to be a turn-on for women?

My friends, my female ones anyway, were convinced that I was going to have to deal with becoming more desirable than I'd ever been in the past (not immensely difficult, I know). They thought I was stupid and naïve not to think that might happen. The idea of being with anyone other than Samantha was so abhorrent to me in the aftermath of her passing that it made little difference anyway, but my chums argued that, as inappropriate as I thought it may be to start a relationship, as women may not see it that way, and that I should be mindful of that fact.

Regardless of my state of mind, I still didn't accept it was true. As much as it sounds like an attractive prospect to be with a man who's proven himself as a husband and father in the past, it comes at a price of huge emotional baggage. Plus, look at it a different way – how attractive a proposition do single mothers present in general? Are they a demographic being overwhelmingly heralded for their desirability? Is parenting competence and an ability to run a home on their own enough to see hordes of men clambering over themselves to chase them?

Still, for some reason, a myth exists that men looking after children is an attractive proposition, even a prerequisite for some women. In reality, there were a few women who let their interest in me be known, but there was far from a steady stream of them, and Britney never, ever called. And who am I to say why they found me irresistible? It could have just been my aftershave.

I think the biggest thing I earned from women was their respect, rather than their phone numbers.

And that's all I wanted.

# 14.
# Teaching the mums a thing or two

How common is it to see a man in sole charge of a child, in particular a baby? Before I found myself in that situation, I am unsure how I would have reacted to the sight of a man carrying a baby around, hauling all the equipment they need for them too.

I'm not a stranger to the concept of a man bag. I'd used one in certain work and travel scenarios when I couldn't be bothered with my briefcase, or if I only needed a few files, flight tickets, and a change of underwear. Mind, having a plush brown leatherette over-the-shoulder number complete with sections for nappies, wipes, thermometer, Calpol, talc, rash cream, nail-clippers, plasters, drinks, waterproofs and leaflets for child-friendly venues was never really part of the plan.

A 'man's man' would only consider a bag necessary if you couldn't carry all your beers and money in your hands and pockets, and even then, carrying a bag is really a woman's job, surely. Yes, bags are for women. Only women should have bags. We have toolboxes and cases for sports equipment, not bags, not us. We're men's men.

Thing is, I've always thought that was bollocks.

It was a particularly common, and prevalent, attitude in the pubs I'd frequent as a young man, and the sports teams I would play in. These were male-dominated places, and a lot of the beliefs voiced were only done so far from earshot of the opposite sex, especially those they were actually in relationships with.

Engaging in any behaviour not judged to be wholeheartedly male meant there must be something wrong with you. Not a healthy stance or attitude, and for many men, I suspect, it was out of much deeper insecurities and fear of the unknown.

I was far from being an active left-wing liberal, campaigning for equality, but I generally did my own thing, and didn't let derision or teasing – bullying even – sway what I chose to do. I can take stick, and I think that's because I'm always keen to dish it out myself, and I'm comfortable enough in my own decision-making to know that someone's harsh words often say more about them than about me.

I guess I have a pretty mixed-bag personality because of my random attitude to different things. Or perhaps it isn't so random. It's that I'm prepared to question the norm a little more than most, without really being a boundary-pusher for the sake of it. Basically, if I like the idea of something, I'll give it a try. For example, I dyed my hair bleach-blonde as a 19-year-old. It was hardly groundbreaking rebellion, I just thought I'd give it a go. The day after I had it done, I turned up for work, and I guess I shouldn't have been surprised by the reaction. The firm I worked for employed about 100 people, manufacturing specialist valves for use on naval equipment and in power plants. I worked in the offices, where the vast majority of the employees came to work every day, suited and booted, and were very serious about their work. So was I, to a point, but I thought my hair colour made no difference to my work at all.

'Backs against the walls, lads,' came the heckles from the shop floor as I clocked in. Some were clearly good-natured, and it was obvious they just thought (rightly) that I was a complete plonker for going for a nearly yellow hairstyle. But others were less comfortable with it, and even stopped talking to me in passing afterwards. In the supposedly more civilised office, there were no heckles, but the managing director, on his regular morning walk around, completely ignored me. Well, he saw me okay, but thought better of a 'good morning'. What I didn't immediately realise was that he went straight to our receptionist to ask who the hell I was. It was a dramatic change of appearance, I grant that, but I was sitting at my own desk, and more than a moment's glance – or passing sniff – would have confirmed that it was me in my chair.

He came back to talk to me, unsure whether my hair wasn't appropriate for work, but we agreed that it didn't affect my ability to do my job.

What I was more interested in was why, a very confident man, one with the keys to the castle (on in this case the company), wasn't able to approach me himself in the first place? He'd have challenged anyone else, or certainly introduced himself to any visitors or new staff we had, even when he didn't know who they were, but my bright lemon hair and

I were different.

I also had to laugh several months later, when a woman in the office went from long, curly auburn hair to a very short, blonde haircut. Without hesitation that morning, she was the first person he spoke to. And what did he say? Yeah, of course. 'I like your hair.'

Now you could say there was absolutely nothing in that, and that the anecdote is completely normal. But that's kind of my point. Men aren't expected to do some things that women are, and vice-versa.

When it comes to parenting, then, what about a man doing it on his own? Are we equipped for it?

I think the undeniable answer – of which I hope to be living proof – is that we absolutely are. There are even advantages to being a man, with certain aspects of childcare coming easier to those of us with scrotums, both in practical terms – shorter queues to the gents' toilets – and emotional ones – we're less concerned about the gossip.

But another truth is that men bringing up children are still in a minority, and while the tide may be turning, it will be a long time before men are automatically assumed to be equal, and for their very presence at a playgroup not to raise a single eyebrow.

Being the token man with a baby somewhere was not without its benefits. In grief, I liked to think my situation was special, and that what I was doing was unusual. Being the only man at a children's group made it feel that way. There was also the fact that folks would be interested in me, and often find kind words for the decisions I'd made. I have never claimed to be any sort of hero, but at the same time I can't say it wasn't nice to hear people say good things about my performance as a parent.

What really meant a lot was when mothers would ask me for advice, or want me to chip in on a discussion they were having about their kids. I guess it's not unusual, or terribly interesting, for people to talk about their children at parenting groups, but it was a welcome surprise when mums turned the tables on me, and instead of me gleaning information, tips and guidance from them, it was me dishing out the parenting wisdom. The first few times it happened, I was looking over my shoulder to double-check they weren't talking to someone behind me.

I don't know why I should be so surprised. We were all in the same situation, regardless of gender, all being the prime care-givers for our children, so I suppose it was only right – natural even – for me to share my ideas, thoughts and experiences, too. Plus, being a man, I would perhaps have a different decision-making process.

I wasn't totally reliant on parenting groups in my quest for quality parenting information. In England, each area has clinics specifically for babies and pre-schoolers. They are run by professionals called Health Visitors, and as their name would suggest, they also visit parents and their children at home.

In the first year of development, you are encouraged to visit these clinics as often as you want. Some parents even go every week, especially if their child has a condition that they want to keep an eye on. One of the things they seem to do as a matter of course is to measure your baby each time you visit. They lay them in the scales, and then measure their height (it's recorded as length for the first twelve months as they don't really stand up at that stage) to check they are developing along a consistent path. I don't know if it is the same everywhere, but each child is issued with their own health record – an A6-sized red book – that keeps all the records of their health, such as immunisation, notes from clinic visits and their measurements. In the back, there are charts that mark average growth, and percentiles of them. For health balance, percentiles should match, so if your child is on the 90th percentile in height (higher than the norm), they should be similar in weight.

As you'd expect with any profession, the Health Visitors can be a little hit and miss. Some you'd feel knew less than you, and others appeared to be the oracle on everything, like there was nothing you could ask that they wouldn't have an answer for.

I did try though. And not because I like being awkward (which I'm not denying either) but because I think my brain operates in a different way to others, and perhaps like the mothers at the playgroups had discovered, I'd come at things from a different angle, posing questions that others wouldn't. Plus in the Internet age, you can be an instant expert on the question you're asking all by yourself – really I'd be checking my information was right, or even testing to see how good the Health Visitor was. I'd also save up the questions I'd like an answer to but that weren't particularly pressing. One of those was about replacing formula milk with cow's milk.

The rule of thumb is that you should wait until a child is one before giving them full-fat milk, which can be changed to semi-skimmed milk once a child turns two. They need the fat or something like that. In this case it has been such a well-trodden practice that parents do it without really thinking any more about it. But not me. I wanted the science, the facts and figures, any consequences of not switching, or the advantages – if there were any – of waiting longer.

Throughout his first two years, my boy was a very good eater. I thought I gave him a very balanced diet, and I wanted that to continue. But the one thing my lazy bugger infant wouldn't do was chew anything tougher than a sausage. This was possibly because I kept mashing his dinners for too long, but in any case, he wasn't getting a lot of meat down his neck. I was a tad concerned about this, and any resulting iron or protein deficiency.

I'd discovered that formula milk, especially the follow-on stuff, was packed with iron, whereas one of the possible negative of cow's milk is it can block some iron absorption. So I pondered whether it would be better, while my boy persisted in his reluctance to chew, that I continued giving him formula milk. I sat with the Health Visitor to discuss the matter. I didn't think it was that complicated. But she sure made a meal of it. In fact, that's what she made me do. 'Talk me through Max's diet,' she said. I proceeded to go through what he ate, which was generally a combination of mashed vegetables and meat, fruit, yoghurt and Red Bull (just kidding, I never did give him yoghurt). I also explained that, while he'd chew sausages, he wouldn't persist with anything tougher, so to try and give him some balance I'd been to a farm shop to get different types of sausage. I got him some beef varieties, some chicken, I think he even had venison.

I didn't mean it to show off. My farm shop visits were always convenient, and usually part of a day trip somewhere. And I didn't think I was pandering to a fussy child who I should perhaps had forced to chew more. It was just providing my boy with a decent diet along the path of least of resistance.

But this health visitor looked stunned, and said: 'Sounds like Max has a very balanced diet. Why are you even asking this question?'

I was getting frustrated. I wasn't looking for praise, I was just looking for an answer, a professional opinion. I never got one. Instead I left, none the wiser, to the comment: 'You could teach the mums a thing or two!'

Now, I think she meant this as compliment, and perhaps that's how I should have taken it. But instead, I took a little exception. 'What do you mean by that?' I asked.

The health visitor was silent.

'I mean it implies that you'd assumed I wasn't capable,' I continued. 'That it's something of a surprise that, as a man, I couldn't even begin to know anything about parenting.'

I left before she could answer me. I'd made my point I hoped. Perhaps it was the frustration of wasting my morning, coupled with my sensitivity about providing my son with a normal upbringing that made me snap. Perhaps I should have just breathed deeply, interpreted her words as kind ones, and walked away. But there is still a bigger part of me that thinks I was right to pull her up, and to make her think about what she had said a bit more carefully.

This certainly was not an isolated incident, and not the only time that I felt that compliments were back-handed insults. But there were other times when I felt torn about responding to comments from well-meaning people.

My best pal and I had children only six months apart, and as he worked shifts, there were days when he was responsible for his daughter. We'd regularly spend a day a week together, normally a Tuesday. It felt like the most natural thing in the world for us, two men, two fathers, who were clearly very much in love with their children. We joined playgroups for a term, we attended parent and child swimming lessons together, took advantage of offers at soft-play centres, as well as just having afternoons at a shopping centre or meeting up at a restaurant for lunch.

What any number of women and children are doing all over the world at any moment in time, with no one batting an eye-lid.

For us it was very different.

For some reason it was common for people to assume we were a gay couple. Why it was easier to believe that two men who clearly had separate responsibility for separate children, closer than a gestation period apart, were a homosexual couple rather than just mates out with their kids was hard to understand. Generally we didn't mind it, and actually had a laugh about it, exploiting any family deals on offer. But it did demonstrate that society in general is still not entirely used to, or comfortable with, a man being the predominant care provider, looking after their children in public, especially in places normally associated with mothers.

There was also the issue I've mentioned before, of playgroups being advertised as 'mother and toddler' rather than 'parent and child'. I never went on a crusade, but I like the fact that my presence forced a few groups into a re-think. It still makes me laugh that I was the reason behind some political correctness.

Yes, moi. Laughing as I write.

At least I knew that, while it may not be everyone's normal, and it wouldn't even have been for us had our situation not changed so devastatingly, my son knows there's nothing wrong with being raised by a man.

By me, no less.

And who wants to be normal anyway?

# 15.
# Feeling sick

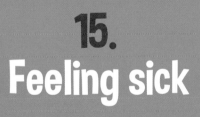

I don't like feeling poorly.

I've got better with age at handling being ill. It isn't all that often that a bug or virus knocks me off my feet, but when it does, I am a little pathetic.

It's the act of *being* sick that I really don't like. When I was little, small but old enough to remember, I was ill into a toilet at home. The toilet was in a room not much bigger than it, with just enough space for you to sit down and shut the door. It meant that no one could join you in there, to hold your hair back, pat your back, or say 'there, there.' Because I couldn't take my mum in with me, I used to kneel with my head over the toilet bowl – I hope you're not reading this chapter at meal time, by the way – lean forward, with one hand on the toilet, and the other stretched out behind me so my mother could hold it as I projectile vomited.

We laugh about it now, and my little sister still jokes that I was about 18 or 19 the last time it happened. Which I'm sure isn't at all true. It was more like 25 I think.

Thing is, I think if you have a particularly boozy adolescence, like I did – when your weekends start from about Wednesday, and your main aim is to see if you can drink more alcohol than you did the previous week – you get somewhat hardened to vomiting. And that meant I couldn't really complain when I felt unwell due to a virus or bug, if I was regularly prepared to make myself ill during weekends of excesses.

The worst I've ever felt physically was shortly after a knee operation when I was 19. I'd managed to rupture my anterior cruciate ligament, quite a serious injury for someone into his sports, or anyone wanting to go up and down stairs in a rush without falling over.

I wasn't overly nervous about the operation, at least until the nurse came to see me shortly before going into theatre. She asked if I had any worries. I said my only fear was for the pain afterwards, which the nurse quickly accepted. 'Yes, there will be pain, but we have all sorts of things we can give you to ease it.' Then she said, 'So you're not worried about waking up during the operation?'

'NOT UNTIL NOW!' I shouted.

Which was the cue for the patient trolley to arrive to take me to theatre.

In the end, I needn't have worried about either. It was the sickness from the anaesthetic I should have been concerned about. It was like nothing else I'd ever experienced in my life. It was nausea on a completely new level. A whole new world of sickness. Makes me queasy thinking about it even now.

When Sam went through childbirth, it was difficult being at her side. But even given the gravity of that situation, it was very different to how you feel watching your little one struggle. Maybe it's a parental instinct, or because you know an infant can't really explain how they feel, or what exactly hurts. Nor can they understand when you tell them that it's going to be okay.

It is daft, but when my child was ill, no matter how mildly, it would send me into a spiral of worry and concern. Like I said, I think I'd been a good foil for Sam when she'd been through various horrible situations. I was there for her when she miscarried, I was the one keeping her calm through childbirth, and I was at her side for every moment I could be when it came to medical treatment for her heart condition. In all those times, while I did worry, it was not ever to the extent of being unable to function, which is how I find myself when my son even has so much as a cough keeping him up at night.

I'm still puzzled as to why I react this way. I'm able to provide what he needs. He gets my love, attention, comfort and medical aid. I even maintain my regular demeanour in front of him, and if he needs cheering up, then I can still play the fool. But inside, I go to pieces. My sense of humour goes out of the window, something that in any other scenario, and I mean any, I've always been able to cling to. I don't sleep. I worry when he's not within eyesight, and I literally get nothing else done.

Can you imagine what I was like when I had to take him to hospital one night?

Yeah, I wasn't good.

Max, at about 18 months old, had been ill for a few days with a nasty cough that was making him wheeze. His nose was regularly getting blocked, and he wasn't very good at blowing it, so his breathing was anything but normal. And it was at its worse as he slept, which he was still able to do intermittently.

We were staying with my sister at that stage, and at about midnight one evening, his breathing had got so bad that I decided it was worth taking him to hospital, to prevent it deteriorating further.

I got everything ready. Max was sleeping in his pyjamas and a fleecy Batman sleepsuit, which was a good combination to take him straight from his cot to his car seat in without major disturbance. He didn't wake up until we arrived at the Accident and Emergency unit of our local hospital, and I put him into a partly reclined pushchair. I had my sister with me; she'd driven us there, and was dutifully staying to help me.

When you're a single parent in certain situations, you really could do with the ability to split yourself in two. In this case I needed to be at my boy's side to re-assure him in strange circumstances and surroundings, but at the same time I needed to speak to the medical staff, as the only one who could give them an accurate account of his medical history.

But I was also used to people making assumptions about our situation. In this particular scenario, we'd arrived at hospital with a young woman driving a young(ish) man and a young boy in the back of a car. It was probably only 'normal' for someone to assume that the woman was the child's mother, and the man his father. That's the assumption the admissions staff made at the hospital, instantly assuming that my sister, Max's aunt, was his mother. They decided to address all their questions to her.

'How long has he been like this?' they asked, and 'Any other conditions or medical history?'

She kept giving the same answer: 'You'll have to ask his dad.' She also then realised that this might make her look like a mother who didn't care, so she explained the relationship among our not very merry trio.

They either weren't listening to her, or didn't take it in, because they continued to address her as Max's mother right until the point he threw up all over himself in his pushchair. Of course, I leapt into action, cleaning him up, changing him into the spare set of clothes I'd brought with us, and comforting him throughout those processes. The penny finally dropped with the medical staff, and they started asking me the questions they needed to.

Deciding that, with his family history and reaction to inhalers, my son could be an asthmatic, and even though there was no immediate concern for Max, the hospital decided to admit him to a ward for monitoring and further treatment.

It was the middle of the night by this time, and I was feeling awful. I was worried sick about Max, even though I knew he was okay in the scheme of things, combined with the stress and exhaustion of missing my usually precious bedtime by a good distance. Emma, bless her, had not gone much farther than my side, and she accompanied us to the ward, helping with Max's bags.

We got to Max's bed, only to be greeted once again by grumpy hospital staff, this time nurses who worked on the ward. After completely dismissing me, a nurse started quizzing my sister for details. Some she knew the answer to, like Max's date of birth, but others she didn't. Again, she directed this nurse to ask me.

The nurse decided to open with, 'But where is his mum?'

'She died when he was seven months old,' I said, expecting a sudden change of attitude.

'I suppose you'll have to do, then,' she said.

Fuck me.

What?

I'll have to do!

My worry, tiredness and stress all instantly turned to passive-aggressive rage – which is something of a forte of mine.

'I suppose I will,' I said. 'In answer to your question, Max Andrew Newbold was born on the 22nd of December at 4.15pm weighing eight pounds, one-and-a-half ounces. He was born by ventouse suction, after his mother – with an epidural administered from about 2.30pm – couldn't manage an unassisted birth. He measured 51cm. Next question.'

'Well, there's no need to be like that,' said my friend the admissions nurse.

'Funny,' I replied. 'I thought your next question might have been a relevant medical one. No, I didn't need to be like that, but I think I've made my point.'

Now a bit stunned, but still not really retreating to an apologetic position, she reverted to the medical questionnaire.

I was proper pissed off. When she'd finished her questionnaire and was about to disappear, I stopped her and asked if she thought it was reasonable for her to instantly write me off. She said there was often no point talking to dads at all. It was always the mums that knew 'this sort of stuff.'

I accepted that, when time was of the essence, it may be normal for medical staff to focus on mothers in children's wards, as they are commonly the main care provider, and thus the source of the child's information. But I also pointed out that even when it was explained to her, twice, that Max's mother had died, she still attempted to address his aunt – a woman – rather than me, his dad.

At this point she asked if I had enough help at home, and that if I didn't, I should consider getting more.

I was fighting a losing battle. This woman had formed an opinion of me, and my attempts to educate her were wasted. I just grinned and tried to stay out of her way.

But it was a situation that kept repeating itself.

Max was in hospital for only 24 hours, but with the regular shift changes, the situation was replayed again and again.

The concerned grandparents had joined us once it had become daylight and I'd let them know. We occupied a little corner of the ward's day room with the sicker children restricted to their beds. It seemed every time someone came to inspect Max, ask a question, or give us some information, I was the last person they looked to speak with.

I've been through some lows after Sam's death. But this situation was the most depressing and gut-wrenching I'd experienced. The feeling of helplessness and worry is bad enough when your child is ill. But to also feel constantly second-class, and be treated like an afterthought by a series of medical 'professionals', made the situation very sad indeed.

It got so predictable that we were making little jokes of it. Emma would generally be the one addressed first, the best guess at being Max's mother. Then they'd try each of the grandmas. And even when it was clearly established who I was, and that it was me who had sole responsibility, partway through conversations the medical staff would start addressing the women in the room rather than me. I'd get the headline news, but when they had something practical to suggest, like 'Try rubbing this on his chest at night', they'd be saying it to his aunt and grandmas.

This poorly boy was put to bed night after night by his dad. Why was that, or is that, so hard to understand?

It's one thing saying it's very honourable for a dad to step up and look after his child full time. Saying it's cute even. But it isn't about that. It isn't a noble thing to do, it's what any sound *parent* would want to do for their child – to provide the best for them, to give them stability, consistency and love.

What I've done, did and am still doing is absolutely not worth one raised eyebrow.

However, it is worth at least one book purchase.

# 16.
# The simple complexity of parenting

How many different types of parent are there?

The strict parents.

The lenient ones.

The ones full of praise.

The ones more willing to criticise.

Those who choose to 'helicopter parent', whatever that means.

I could go on, but I won't.

I believe if there are 6 billion parents on earth, then that's how many different types of parenting there will be. We all do it differently. There is no right and wrong, there is no grey line – more a permanent misty haze and kaleidoscope of colour.

Did I think I'd make a good parent? Well, yes. Because I'm of the often misguided belief that I can put my mind to, and be brilliant at, anything I choose to (apart from modesty). But what does being a good parent actually mean?

Before becoming a father I didn't pay a huge amount of attention, or grant a great deal of respect, to the world's parents. A failing of mine as an individual, really, that I couldn't empathise with those who had children, or even care enough to try.

In my full-time working days, I had something of an ivory tower existence. I used to have a huge office, big enough for a twelve-seat conference table as well as my electrical height-adjustable desk. If you'd said I was a little single-minded, I would struggle to put up much of an argument. I wasn't quite the dictator type at work, but I didn't much care to get to know people past the jobs they had to do.

And that's not what I saw parenting as anyway – a job, really? Just how difficult could it be? It's all coffee and daytime television. Granted, it's sure to be boring, but difficult? Nah, give me a break.

At that time, parenting just seemed to me like an interruption to everything else, and while I certainly sympathised with mums and dads, especially when they had a poorly child, I didn't really think they ever had it hard. Of course, I understood it could play merry havoc with a person's emotions, but the actual physical acts of looking after children didn't seem overly complicated to me.

How complicated can something be if it comes without instructions?

Well, even more complicated than putting together an IKEA wardrobe, I can – now – tell you.

There is so much to know if you are to be an effective and loving parent, so much conflicting information to dissect and apply to your own situation, decisions for the shortterm that affect the longer term. There are a million variables to consider in your decision-making, and lots that could undo the good work of a few years in just a few moments.

I don't claim to be the world's best dad (everyone knows that's Peppa Pig's dad) but am comfortable in the knowledge I am regularly doing my best. which I think is the first lesson of being a quality parent.

## Always give your child your best.

This advice is completely open to misinterpretation, so I will try for some elaborate clarification.

What I don't mean by 'your best' is that every day has to be unforgettable for your child, that they wake up to a well-planned, daily adventure out, nor do I mean they get 100% of your attention, permanently. The reality is that no one gives 100% all the time. It isn't possible, or even desirable, to try to operate at that level for a sustained period of time. It only leads to burn out and ultimately making mistakes, or sacrifices that return long-term losses on the premise of short-term gains.

Children should come first, and get your best, but sometimes that actually means stepping back.

A parent needs to retain an identity – to be available for their child as and when necessary, but also to be wary of focusing solely on them, at a detriment to themselves. You actually owe it to your child to show them the world revolves around more than one person, and that at times it is totally normal they aren't a priority. I like the dramatic comparison of a paramedic attending a serious road traffic accident. I mean, when medics talk about attending car crashes, and training others for them, they say it's not the ones who are screaming you need to help first, it's the ones not making any noise. A child might say, 'I was shouting for you and you never came, instead you went into the kitchen,' to which you may reply, 'Indeed. I needed to turn down the heat on the stove, otherwise I'd have burnt your food. Then I'd have had less time to play with you as I'd have needed to clean up the mess. Sometimes you have to wait.'

**Put yourself in their shoes.**
When Samantha died, I regularly used this technique to help me make, and justify, decisions. If I was struggling to come up with an answer to a conundrum, or which path to tread, I would reverse our situation, and think how I'd have liked Sam to proceed if I was the absent one. It wasn't always for important calls. It was more for little things, like deciding where to take Max that day.

This is a practice I have continued in a different way – by putting myself into my son's shoes to help me make a decision. There is a twist, though, as I don't try to put myself in his shoes today, as a child. Instead I try to imagine what he would think as an adult. For example, if he's asking me for another ice-cream after just finishing one, I wouldn't put myself in his young shoes for the answer, because of course it will be yes. Instead, I try to think if his adult self would thank me for always saying yes to requests for unhealthy things.

That's perhaps too dramatic, and simplistic, an example, but I hope that explains my point. It will differ from situation to situation, from question to question, and sometimes it does help to put yourself in their shoes as they see it now. Things that you see no relevance in can be very important to a child.

**Consistency, consistency and more of the same.**
When Samantha was pregnant with Max, the one piece of advice I kept hearing was routine, routine, routine. Children thrive on knowing what is

coming and on having firm boundaries.

It's certainly true with babies and toddlers. You can physically see the benefits of them knowing where they stand, and what is coming next. It helps them learn positive behaviour, and what constitutes the opposite.

Having regular meal times and sleep patterns can play a good part in developing a healthy lifestyle for your children. Having a body clock that doesn't know when it should be awake or asleep, or a stomach that yearns for sustenance at differing times of the day, can lead to confusion and bad habits. Developing good ones in childhood can set a person up for a healthier lifestyle in adulthood.

There's also a benefit to parents. You too know what is coming, and can plan to fit in other things you want to get done around the routine. You know that if your child is regularly asleep at a certain time, not only are they likely to have had enough rest for a successful day tomorrow, but you are also freed up from that time in an evening for tasks that are too difficult to do when your child is awake.

**Never change your mind, even if you are wrong.**

There have been times when I know I've made the wrong call. I can't remember too many specifically, but I do know there have been occasions where, retrospectively, I would have made a different decision. Perhaps my child asked me for a treat, and I've said no, when in reality he'd been good, demonstrated positive behaviour all day, eaten well. But mindful of a previous treat, I'd turned down his request. I may have instantly regretted this decision, and thought it would have been better to grant him his requested reward, but it is still important to stick to your guns. You can even explain that to a child if you want.

As a baby turns into a toddler they will automatically start to question you more, and when they get into the terrible twos, they push you, just to check that you are up to the task. That's what it feels like anyway. They won't ask once for something, they will ask until they think you'll cave in, or until something else distracts them. Sometimes their demands can last all day, or for several days.

On these occasions, I would retort with, 'Has Daddy ever changed his mind?'. This is not an instant fix for a young child to understand, and to stop them asking for things, but it certainly helps. And over time it means that if they can't answer that question with an example, they give up more easily and quickly than they did before.

**Try to see the bigger picture.**

Lots of parenting is reactionary, of course – you see your child heading for something, or instantly presenting you with a new challenge, and you have to make a call on the spot.

But it can pay to think a little more about the situation you are in before making a judgement and wading in. Obviously a lot of things require your immediate attention, and intervention, but even at these times it is wise to take a moment, or pause for an interim action.

I can recall one instance when I took Max to his reception class. In the ten minutes they assign the children to play before they go in for the day, Max was running around with his friends. I was in the usual gaggle of parents, waiting on the sidelines with his bag for him to line up to go into the classroom. I could see he was enjoying a game of tag, or chasing his mates, but there was one child more keen on interrupting their play than joining in. He was physically holding those playing the game, putting them in distress, but they were largely ignoring him. Then he tried to wrap himself round my son's neck one more time, and in attempting to brush him off, Max caught him with a stray arm. He didn't notice, but this set the other child off in floods of tears, and he headed straight to the teacher on playground duty.

Now, not having witnessed the events unfold, this teacher was presented with an upset child, who had a simple story about Max striking them. The teacher then summoned Max and told him off for hitting this child. This upset my boy, partly as I think he was confused, and mostly as he doesn't like being in trouble. I wasn't the only one who saw what happened, and I was soon encouraged by other parents to intervene. 'I wouldn't be having that,' and 'That's really unfair, are you going to say anything?' they said. And I did have words, but they were only for my child.

I didn't see much point in offering him an excuse, or explaining the series of events to the teacher. Instead, I chose to use it as an opportunity to teach my child something else – that life is unfair sometimes.

He needs to know that he has my support, but he also needs to know that sometimes people will make unjust decisions, or do things you feel are unjust. If I'd just stepped in and perhaps righted a wrong, that's not a lesson he would have got, and perhaps would have learned very little from that event.

### Explain things and talk to them.

'You can tell he's been talked to,' was something I'd always be confused to hear. Of course I talked to my child. Didn't everybody?

Actually they meant something entirely different. Parents can often dumb down what they are saying to a child, or neglect to talk to them at all about a subject, assuming that they'd not be able to understand. But it doesn't need to be that way. I'm not saying that as parents we don't need to adapt our language when talking to a child, but unless you do talk to a child, how can you help expand their language knowledge and vocabulary?

I think the Mr Men series of books, written by the late Roger Hargreaves, are excellent examples of the language that can engage a young mind. The stories are brilliant and often use challenging words, as well as using a series of different words with the same meaning. I'm no Mr Hargreaves, but I like to think that by being as eloquent as I can be in front of my child, he will only benefit.

### Seek help and advice – reciprocate when you can.

Parenting advice comes in all sorts of forms, from all sorts of resources

– books, magazine articles, newspapers, websites, health professionals, other parents.

It can be very annoying when you feel like you are struggling, while others around you seem to parent effectively and effortlessly. Even worse, there are those all too ready to point out where you are going wrong, and what you could be doing better.

Well, here's what you are doing wrong and what you could be doing better.

Not really.

Organic learning, or learning by osmosis, are terms I like to use. I've not picked up too many parenting books, and none that I've followed to the absolute letter, but that doesn't mean I haven't got a great deal from resources like that. I'm also occasionally partial to a TV programme that looks at how to help with kids' behaviour. But for me, by far the best means of gaining valued advice has been talking to other parents. There would be some parents I'd listen to intently, albeit for very different reasons. Some would appear to be brilliant at looking after their children, so I'd be listening to them to get any tips to replicate at home. Others I'd carefully listen to, so I could make sure I didn't follow their advice.

That may read a little sinister, but it's not meant to! I just think parenting is all about learning and paying attention.

I'd also look at people who had children in the next clear stage of development – so when my boy was crawling, I'd look at parents with walkers for guidance. It made sense to be prepared for what was coming.

And it wasn't a one-way street. I liked to share my experiences and ideas with others too. I don't like to feel like I'm lecturing (that has probably been the most difficult thing in writing this book), but when you are sharing your experiences, it doesn't feel like that, even if people take what you tell them and apply similar tactics with their own children.

**Persevere and be patient.**

Before I was a parent, I didn't think I had much patience, and I still don't with certain things. But it's absolutely vital when it comes to looking after children, if you want to remain calm anyway. Sometimes they need things to be explained a lot of times before they get them, and there are times it's of benefit to wait for them to do things, rather than getting them done quickly yourself.

It's one of my identified failings as a parent. When we were getting ready to go out of a morning, I'd dress him, put his shoes on the right feet and zip up his coat to save time, and face, especially if leaving it all to him would have meant we'd be late. But in the longer run, it would have been much better if I'd been patient, or allowed more time in our schedule for him to do more for himself.

There are also times when I know I'm going to have to dig in, and put up with some pain, in order to grant myself a longer-term win. Like the introduction and use of the naughty step. Making a child take a time out (a minute for each of their years in age) can be a daunting thing to begin with. You may feel like your little treasure is never going to sit still when you put them down for a couple of minutes, and the idea of trying to get them to do so is enough to put you off trying. But I've seen it work for my own child, and I've seen it work for others. It doesn't happen without some hard work, but the long-term benefits can save a whole lot of time in the longer run. For example, my boy would have to be put on a step what felt like hundreds of times (probably more like twenty) before he'd sit still and contemplate why I'd put him there, but he did get used to it, and understand it. Eventually I remember a time when I think he threw something, one of his toys perhaps, and instantly he knew what he'd done was wrong. 'Should I go sit on the naughty step, Dad?' he asked me. That may very well have been the last time he threw something in anger.

**Put more in and get more out.**

At times it can feel like your life is about nothing other than your children. Far from letting that thought consume you, your best course of action may actually be to do even more for them. I've always found the more I've put in – the more effort I've made, the more things I've done – the more my child has responded, and the more I felt I got out of parenting myself.

Parents, myself included, often rightfully claim to be knackered, and if you feel that way you might be thinking I'm mad to suggest doing more, but that's exactly what I am suggesting. Some days I'd be so tired I fancied staying at home, doing little more than playing around the house, cleaning and feeding him at the appropriate times. But this was a vicious, self-defeating circle. The less stimulated my child was, the worse his behaviour became, and the harder it was to administer his care. By actually planning more, fighting tiredness with getting ourselves out and about doing things, no matter how much I initially felt like I'd rather be doing the opposite, the benefits were huge. Max was much easier, and more entertaining, on days where we'd been out and positive, rather than when we tried to have a 'lazy' day at home. I would still be tired, but a much more manageable tired. I had more energy, and most importantly I maintained a very healthy enthusiasm for parenting.

## Take a break and press reset.

Looking after children can become all-consuming. Young kids will rarely show that they appreciate the job you're doing, and it can feel like a thankless task. All parents deserve a break if they can get one. As well as being refreshing and energising, I've found that breaks can act as a kind of parenting reset button. It would be fantastic if children came with remote controls – I'm sure the volume down and mute buttons would be well worn on most controllers – but sadly they don't just yet. I've always found when I get a decent break from my son, though, when he goes off for time with his grandparents, for example, I notice different things about his behaviour and development when he comes back. It also sometimes makes it clear that I need to do more or less of a certain thing, or when my ideas are or aren't working.

## Ignore everyone and do what feels right to you.

Trust your instincts and ignore everyone, including me, especially me.

Make mistakes and learn from them.

We are only superhuman, after all.

# 17.
# Putting me on hold

Max was a baby, but he wouldn't be forever. I knew in a couple of years he'd start going to nursery, and only a couple after that he'd be at school and in full-time education. Given the loss he'd suffered, and his importance to me, it didn't even seem comparable to think about what I might 'lose' by doing little other than look after him for four years or so, compared to what he might gain by having me at his side throughout his pre-school years.

As it happens, my job had always been an interruption to the other things I actually wanted to do in my life. Granted, I was good at what I did, and handsomely paid, meaning that more of those things were financially possible, but it was never a calling, or something I'd consider getting out of bed for without the chunky pay cheque due every month.

In my varied professional pursuits I'd put a fair amount of effort into looking at different careers, or certainly at different job functions. I'd eliminated retail, not wanting to regularly sacrifice weekends of sport and socialising. I'd discounted manual labour on the basis of instability, and the risks of self-employment in a field where injury would mean a loss or earnings, or even complete career. And in the field I did choose, office-based work, I'd concentrated on what I was good at, and what paid the best, requiring the least amount of effort. I'd travelled the lucrative path of least resistance. And if you put that sentence into any job suitability questionnaire, you'd have got my job – you'd have got me.

I know I'm not unusual in working in a field I had no passion for or got no enjoyment from. I imagine the vast majority of people go to work with dread rather than joy in their hearts. It's a means to an end – a rather nice end, but an unfortunate means all the same.

Leaving full-time work to care for Max meant I was effectively giving up the means to a life I didn't have any more. Samantha had died, and our life together was gone, too. Money that I'd have earned and perhaps used for a bigger mortgage, a nicer car, foreign holidays or other material things had become even more unnecessary than it was before. We'd always been pragmatic, but perhaps along more indulgent lines before. Sharing nice things together meant a lot to us, then. Now those things seemed completely unimportant.

It was time to take stock. If my life was on hold, it would only be on hold for a relatively short amount of time. This devastating loss was presenting itself as an opportunity to grasp hold of things that, had things remained equal, would not have entered much more than a day dream.

To be fair, the exponents of the phrases 'you'll need to do your own thing' and 'you'll destroy yourself if you're *just* looking after Max' had a point, although I'm not sure they actually knew what it was. I did agree that I needed more in my life than 'just' Max. As immense as that boy continues to be, I accepted it wouldn't be healthy for him to be my permanent sole focus. It wouldn't be good for me, and it certainly wouldn't be good for him. Folks outside our situation were focused on me, as I think they do for mothers who seem too involved in their children in the months after their arrival. But there would also have been long-term effects on my child.

I think people would have found it excusable for me to hide behind my son, to take practical comfort in his care, and to be frightened of anything different, perhaps living vicariously through my child from then on. But it wasn't something I was prepared to excuse myself for. As much as I was dependent on my child, I didn't want that to become a permanent situation, and I certainly didn't want the opposite to occur, where my child became completely dependent on me.

It is absolutely true that I was completely dependent on him in the hours, days, weeks and months directly following Sam's death. Eventually the level of my dependence dwindled to what it is today – I need him around to operate at my absolute best, but not to be able to function, or to find a desire for life.

Sam used to romanticise and daydream about our family's future, when our children were all grown up. She'd set scenes of being invited to their houses for dinner, and in her more whimsical moments, to babysit our grandchildren. I didn't want to rain on her parade so I didn't tell her off for her fantasies, but I did often remind her that our children would be their own people, and the choices they made in life could be very different to the ones we had chosen. Not only did we need to be ready for that, we needed to actively encourage them to follow their own dreams and passions. My sentiments often fell on deaf ears, but it was a drum I'd have continued to beat, I'm sure.

I'm not saying it's easy to do, or natural even, but I do strongly believe that it is the definition of sound parenting. Breeding people who are comfortable in their own skin and mind, who know that they are loved and wanted, but feel free to follow their hopes and aspirations, wherever they may take them.

But what were my hopes and aspirations now?

As a family unit, Samantha, Max and I had a vague life plan – nothing formally written down, but something in our heads, about how our future was going to be financed, and perhaps where I saw us living. With Samantha now gone, that plan was in pieces, and initially it was far too painful for me to think about planning a future without her. Plans were made on an hourly basis, then perhaps a day or two ahead, but always on a practical front. I was never really thinking about myself, or my personal development. I had to learn to be a full-time single parent. That was going to be a big enough job as it was (and the pay and prospects were rubbish).

Through some sound financial planning and saving, by eventually being made redundant from work, then living with family, cutting back on virtually every expense to the bare minimum, the one thing I did buy myself was time – time to concentrate on being a dad. As difficult, or different, as my life had suddenly become, I was in a decent financial position. I couldn't go and do whatever I pleased, but certainly I was not in a position where I would be forced to work as long as I lived on a strict budget. It could have been a lot worse, and as stressed as I got at times, I didn't suffer from the burden of excessive money worries, or concerning myself with putting a roof over our heads or food on the table.

Time passed, and while I still found looking into the future troublesome and not without pain, I did start to formulate a new and lucid personal life plan, and a time frame to go with it. I had two years until Max would start to go to nursery, and another two before he'd start school full-time. These became significant points in the informal five-year plan for both of us. I budgeted to have enough to last all those years on a figurative shoestring, without my having to do much more than an effective job of parenting. However, any time that I could afford myself would be used to put actions in place that would have me back on my professional feet by the time my boy put on a school uniform. There would be snippets of time for me to think about work in his pre-nursery years, then I'd naturally have more time as he started nursery, then once at school everyday I'd almost have full workdays back to myself before even considering additional childcare (something I've never really done).

If I could get back to work and generate an income, it would mean some of the savings I now intended to spend as an income could stay savings. But what would I do?

Sam's death had such a dramatic effect on my mind – on its ability to concentrate and remember things, as well as on my feelings about getting stuck in the rat race again. Life was far too short for Samantha. Wouldn't it be an insult to her life for me to hop back into a career path I never cared much for before she died?

I was learning a lot of things about myself all the time. I'd always valued my ability to put things into perspective and prioritise, and that had most definitely sharpened. Max had his part to play in that too, of course. I couldn't quite believe the range and intensity of emotions my little boy would put me through, just by completing the simplest of tasks. He was amazing, but at the same time no different to any other child. I loved being with him, and couldn't think of anywhere else I'd rather be, or anything that could be any more important. If I'd been passionate about my career, doing something I felt born to do, perhaps it would have been different. But being Max's dad felt like a calling, a purpose, the most important job in the world. I would raise a wry smile at those in very well-paid jobs who'd get upset, angry and stressed about something that had frustrated them at work. There were celebrities and sports stars being widowed with children, and it would puzzle me as to why they remained in the public eye, and effectively at work, rather than at home with their kids. Surely they had enough money to allow them to do that? It was different for me with a baby, and perhaps it would have been different if Max had been older when his mother died, but still it took me a good while to even consider the positions taken by other people in not dissimilar circumstances. Perhaps I needed a passion?

I forced myself to really think about my ideal career, and I came up with an anonymous Formula One racing driver, a pseudonym-bearing writing phenomenon, chief taster at the Swizzels Matlow sweet factory, and a fighter pilot. I also quite fancied giving chimney sweeping a go.

Flying and writing were the only two fields that were realistic. Training to become a pilot is a serious and costly business, though, and doesn't really recommend itself for life as a single parent. Mind you, Max could probably have fit into an overhead locker for a good few years yet. I did take one helicopter lesson to see how much it would whet my appetite for being airborne and in control, and while it was good fun, the desire just wasn't there. Plus, when I came to hover by some of my family, who had come to view my lesson, the sight of Max screaming and in uncontrollable tears was a further prod not to take it any further.

I researched a other career options, too. Physiotherapy is one I remember looking at. But again the training seemed lengthy, rigorous, costly, and ultimately was something I'd have to put a lot of time into, time I didn't have, or may regret not using to some other end.

Writing interested me. It was a harsh world, but a varied one. And critically one that could be done remotely, on a freelance basis, to slot alongside being a single parent dad. Which is pretty much where I started, writing about my experiences with Max.

The best piece of advice I got was to start a blog, and to choose a subject I'd have plenty to write about. Being a man bringing up a baby alone, I had the perfect topic. It is a relatively rare situation, and with children presenting new challenges all the time, it was a subject that I hoped would evolve with my writing. So I started writing at Single Parent Dad, with the sole objective of simply practising my craft. The subject matter was whatever I deemed the most significant events of recent days and I blogged when I could. It was great, as there was absolutely no pressure. I was writing what I wanted, when I wanted.

I knew I was writing in a public domain, where anyone with an Internet connection could read my stuff, but I hadn't really thought through the possible implications of that. There were a few people reading my blog from the start, but I called them my grammar police. I asked them to point out any errors or spelling mistakes I was making, and to give me general feedback on how easy – or difficult – they found my posts to read. I didn't really ask for comment on the topics or subjects I was covering. I just wanted feedback on my writing ability and style.

It's difficult to remember how long it went on like that, but eventually others found my blog and started leaving me comments. Then a guy called Dan Hughes wrote a blog post about me, and I had a sudden increase in visitor numbers. His blog, All That Comes With It, was very popular in the UK. As a novice, I had no idea that someone like him would take an interest in me, and by doing so, what sort of journey it would send me on. He opened my eyes to the blogging world and its many, many, many contributors and realms. I got recommended to other blogs and bloggers, as well as discovering a new world for myself in the rabbit warren that is online writing. The blog developed a life of its own, and ended up providing me much more than just a place to practise. It was a place to make friends, find guidance and advice, and I even started to use it to help me make decisions.

I also completed a distance learning course, from the London School of Journalism. It was delivered in interesting and deliverable sizes, and was the first thing I ever found myself doing for enjoyment, that I may actually one day get paid to do. The freelance writing course gave me a little insight into what life as a writer might be like. I networked with other students and experienced journalists, and I think, given my circumstances, people were always willing to give me the time of day, whilst remaining objective abut my writing acumen. I got some fantastic advice and insights. It was reasonably clear to me that I'd never make a fully-fledged journalist. I just didn't have the zest, or the actual writing skill, for an increasingly competitive, scrutinised field. But I did find that people enjoyed reading what I was writing online, and I found writing gigs that suited my abilities and circumstance. It was work that was never going to make me rich, but I was enjoying it, and it opened doors to meeting new and exciting people and projects.

I am incredibly pleased that I started scribing my thoughts and experiences online. I've met some wonderful people as a result of it, not all in person, but some who I am sure will remain friends for a long time. It has presented me with some great opportunities; if I'd never taken the decision to try my hand at writing, then you wouldn't be reading this (assuming you still are … hello, hello? Testing one, two, three?)

But the thing I am most grateful for is the fact that I believe it has made me a better parent – and even a better person.

# 18.
# The hardest job in the world

Any job is as hard as you make it.

Is that true?

There are people operating in any number of capacities that make what they are doing for a living, for necessity or out of choice, look ridiculously easy. They are the envy of their peers. People desperately want to be them, to emulate their apparent success and lack of stress, but is it all just a ruse? Who really has it toughest?

When I was a child, even as a young man, my dad generally came home from work in an absolutely foul mood. The other members of our family unit – my mother, my sister and I – would often change our behaviour to try and ease him back into the mild, friendly and kind man we all knew he was underneath. It was a delicate business, and obviously at different ages and times we, as children, didn't really appreciate the situation or act in a way to help. We'd deliberately do the opposite of what was needed. We got kicks out of winding him up.

Thing is, I think we all thought my dad had it very tough at work because of how he'd be when he arrived home from the office. He was the managing director of a firm that made car parts. They were on a near permanent 24-hour shift with over 200 employees, trying to maintain high levels of quality with products being delivered just in time to car plant production lines, demands varying by the hour. On top of that, he was chairman of a parent company that owned a number of other firms. He was a busy man, he was a very well-paid man, he was an important man.

Whereas my mother was at home. She had the easy job of looking after us kids. We were no trouble. There was just my sister, who couldn't complete a piece of homework without taking a few doors off their hinges, and me, who would barely admit to having homework, let alone do it, and would dirty at least two sets of clothes a day, one at school and one playing out in the garden or down at the cricket club.

Easy.

So easy that as we got older my mother returned to a full-time teaching post at our high school. She had so much time, you see, she'd be better off at work, and blimey, is teaching much of a job? They get a million weeks of holiday a year or something. Life's a breeze for a full-time teaching parent of two isn't it?

When Max was born, he interrupted some of our rituals and routines. Sam and I had always finished work at similar times, and would generally spend the journey home talking to one another about how our respective days had gone, as well as what we'd be having for tea. First home starts cooking, that sort of thing.

With the birth of our child, that was one thing that stopped. I'd call Sam from my car on the journey home, generally to be told she'd not got time for a chat. Or she'd not even pick up the phone. Too busy? What the hell had she been doing all day? I'd been at work, real work, and she'd been gallivanting at a playgroup, library, swimming baths or shopping centre. If I could find the time to call her, I was sure that she could find the time to talk to me.

'Looking after Max isn't easy, you know,' she'd say.

'Really?' I'd reply. 'He eats the same things at pretty much the same times, can't move from where you leave him and finds jangling keys to be fascinating entertainment. Yeah, real ball-breaking stuff.'

Our arguments, or discussions, were good-natured, and a lot of what we said was meant in jest, but we were in a perpetual argument about who was working harder. I guess it is far from uncommon for partners to argue about this sort of stuff, and to be under the impression that they are the most hard done by in any relationship. But still, I'd be aggrieved to think I'd been 'at work' all day, and I'd still regularly have to come home and cook our dinner, as Sam had not found the time to do it.

And this was despite me spending three or four weeks at home before going back to full-time work. I should have understood that, whilst not being completely debilitated by the birth of a child, you are somewhat thwarted from going wherever and whenever you want. You need to be organised, and a tiny baby comes with a car boot full of 'vital' accessories and aids. Simple processes like making a cup of tea can seem monumental when you are also caring for a baby who seemingly can't be left to his own devices for enough time to boil a kettle, or will distract you so much that you forgot you boiled the water in the first place.

When there are two of you at home, it makes all these tasks really easy. One of you can be 'left holding the baby' while the other gets the necessary tasks in hand. That could just be getting stuff into the car to allow you all to go out, or it could be to cook something for you adults.

And what is life like as a single parent?

It's easy of course.

That much is abundantly clear to anyone who's ever paid any attention to the depiction of our role in the media, or the social stigma associated with it.

Single parents, or should I say single mothers, are a phenomenon to be discouraged, pilloried and eradicated by the rest of us. They are single-handedly (worst pun ever?) responsible for all that is wrong with the world. These are the people raising the unruly, the criminals, the blights we could well do without, and they have the cheek to do it all out of the pockets of the rest of us, on welfare handouts.

And when Samantha died, I became one of them.

I was reluctant to accept the moniker of single parent to begin with. I'm not entirely sure why, I guess because the vast majority of people parenting in that situation haven't found their way there through bereavement. They've mostly got there through a relationship break-up. Things like that are not easy to deal with, when parents no longer wish to be together. Having to try and manage a new type of relationship with someone you once loved, but no longer do. Now finding yourself trying to agree on things in the best interests of your children, and balancing all the variables that brings. Not easy. But not the same as being widowed.

I wanted to feel different, to feel a little special compared to the norm, so I'd rarely call myself a single parent. I'd always tick the widowed box when form filling, rather than the single one. It was a small and pointless mercy that I was unlikely to be derided for 'getting myself into this situation' – it wasn't the fault of Sam or I, or the brilliant National Health Service (and I really bloody mean that, the NHS is the number one reason to live in Britain). If we'd fallen out, people could have argued that our possible future incompatibility was predictable (and look who gets hurt the most, your child, you selfish idiots).

In our, or my case, that didn't happen.

But I was still left holding the baby alone.

Now, of course there are positives to this situation. I would now be free to get my own way on all the parenting decisions. Diet, routine, clothes, brand of nappy, general boundaries and parenting ethos.

Sam and I didn't really disagree on all that much – she would perhaps argue that I was a little too practical, and I would perhaps argue that she'd be led to decisions by how they made her feel, rather than thinking it through properly for our child. I think this made for a good balance. This even continued after she died. I would think of Samantha, discuss things with her, even though she wasn't there, and come to decisions at times of change.

These discussions went on in my head, and would always make me smile. We'd disagree, and Sam would come up with things that I hadn't thought of. It was comforting to think I knew her that well, even in my subconscious, that I could have these impromptu confabs about our child.

But ultimately it was up to me. And when I'd choose a route that I didn't think Sam would have readily agreed with, I had to have greater justification, I had to be able to convince myself that I was doing the right thing. In this way, even after her passing, Samantha made me a better parent.

Yet single parenting proved to be a ridiculous retina-opener.

It certainly wasn't impossible, and my knack for being organised and looking for efficiencies in absolutely everything served me well. Because I want the easiest possible life, I am motivated to constantly find the best way of doing things, meaning I claw back time for other things, other things I'd rather be doing. Like nothing, for example. As a sole parent, the opportunity to do nothing is a rare one. You even have to plan that.

So being super-organised wasn't a problem. Through either my actions or my child's temperament we had a very regular routine, with some flexibility built in, but pretty much always operating to the same basic daily framework. Naps during journeys, being in the right places for easy lunch and dinner times, loading the car with the right props, and having things that served a dual purpose as much as possible. A bottle of water could be used as that until it was drunk, for example. It then could be used as a bath toy, or as to clean shampoo from hair, or even as an emergency urinals for toddlers.

That said, you can be as efficient as you want, but you'll still never be far from busy. Simple chores become ridiculously difficult.

I understood now why Sam couldn't take my early evening calls on the drive home from work. I'd be lucky if I could find my phone when it rang, let alone answer it.

Does all this read like a complaint? A lengthy one about how hard being a single parent is?

I hope not. I'm merely trying to point out that it's one area where perception does not match up to reality. Parents doing a brilliant job of raising their children alone are not recognised enough.

It would always make me giggle a little when someone would say how much of a difficult time they were having at work, and that they were jealous of how easy I had it looking after a child. I'd agree totally, and then point out that if I didn't do my job, then a child would end up neglected, first, malnourished, unwell, underdeveloped and unloved.

Being supposedly free to choose our routine, and not contracted to be anywhere in particular at any point of time, family and friends would occasionally ask me to help them out with stuff at home. 'We're having a carpet fitted, would you mind being around to let them in?' or 'There's a parcel coming to ours some time on Wednesday, can you sit in and wait for it?'

Sure, no bother. I'll change what we're doing. Whatever is it couldn't have been important enough for you to direct a parcel to somewhere you would actually be, or to arrange to arrive late for work one day.

My sarcasm and reluctance certainly started a few debates. And people would – wrongly – often put my behaviour down to grief, and 'excuse' me for it. The reality was I meant a lot of what I said, and still do. It's all too easy to get absorbed in the environment you are in, especially a work one, to think that you have it tough and that what you are doing is all-important. It almost seems natural for anyone in paid employment to think they are more important than those who are merely looking after children. I'm not sure I'm going to be doing a lot to change that, and while people live in ignorance, whose problem is that really?

What I am saying is that I know the truth.

And I have the lack of sleep to prove it.

# 19.
# My mini-colossus

If you could wave a magic wand, borrow the DeLorean time machine from the *Back to the Future* films, and whisk yourself off to a point in the past, where would you go and what would you change?

If I had a pound for every time I've heard 'If I could have my time again …' Well, I'd probably be no better off. For me, it would be better to get paid per cliché written. My point is that people have regrets, reflect on the past, and wish that they had done things differently. Hindsight is indeed a wonderful thing (I should be playing cliché bingo).

Today I find myself barely recognisable as the person I was when Sam died. I liked that person, that 28-year-old me – enough to tread the horribly uncomfortable writing style of the third person. He was a nice guy. He'd worked hard, been very lucky too, but carved himself out a nice professional existence that afforded him all the luxuries he supposed he'd ever really care for. His family supported him, he had some great friends he enjoyed drinking and socialising with. Playing sports at their sides and as part of a team had (almost) always put a smile on his face.

There was a beautiful woman in his life he'd somehow managed to land. She really was amazing. And his life had been further blessed with the safe and healthy arrival of a beautiful boy, Max. Max by name, Max by nature.

He was set for a life of unspectacular bliss.

Then Samantha died.

I've heard stories of people being in denial for weeks, months, even years after a loss, but for me the difficult thing was the initial jolt to the system, the fact that someone I'd planned to spend the rest of my life with had suddenly gone. That can take a little while to absorb. I can recall, in vivid and horrific detail, the graphic process of Samantha losing her life. These are memories I wish to erase and never forget at the same time. I've never been hit by a truck, a car or heavyweight boxer, but I have a suspicion the way I felt witnessing my wife pass away means that, if I ever was, I'd be prepared for how it feels.

I definitely wasn't in denial, though. It was quickly apparent to me that the life I had before was gone and I had a job at hand. I had a baby to look after. A baby who was blissfully unaware of what had just gone on, and what he had lost.

My son needed me.

What he couldn't know is that I needed him more.

Of the two of us, it was more often my boy who was the rock for us to base our life on. I was supposed to be the one he relied on. When he needed changing, I had to be there, armed with nappies, wipes, creams and a smile. When he needed feeding, I had to have cooked and mashed his food, and be on the end of the spoon – or food-delivering aeroplane. When he was tired, I needed to be there to help him settle, to make him comfortable, to get his layers right, and get him off to sleep. When he was upset I needed to work out why, to burp him when he needed it, to amuse him when he was bored, to get the food and drink he thought he was lacking, or even be the one to tell him that his crying was unnecessary. I needed to get this all right.

And it may sound ridiculous, but I couldn't have done any of it without him.

I could 100% rely on him for everything I deemed important. If I needed a lift, he would smile, or do something for the first time. If I needed a distraction, he'd provide one. If I needed something to do in the middle of a dark night, he'd wake. If I needed dragging out from a moment of self-pity, he would be an instant prompt. If I was feeling a little sad, he'd reassure me I was doing the right thing, and also be available for his own particular brand of affection. It might have been him holding my hand when no one else's would do, or using me as a kind of climbing frame when he thought I was the most interesting thing to try and scramble over.

I don't think he could have known the positive effect he was having on his very wounded dad. He wasn't the antidote to grief, but he was the strongest possible medicine.

That's one of the things I was desperate – and still am – for him to understand.

He was always the biggest of blessings. Samantha and I were so delighted with him. His arrival completed our family circle and brought us all closer together, to a new level of relationship intensity. It was a ring of protection, purpose and love, and Max made that possible. Without him, life just wouldn't be as rich, or as worth living. That is his superpower – to give us everything, without ever having to do a single thing. I hope that's a feeling all parents get from their children.

But part of me was concerned that Max wouldn't feel that love in return, or wouldn't understand his importance to me, his one surviving parent. I had this horrible fear that he could actually harbour feelings of being a burden. I'd read lots of things about children blaming themselves for parents falling out, thinking they were the reason behind, for example, their parents' divorce, and I didn't want our situation to draw out similar feelings in my son.

Part of the reason why I didn't return to full-time work after Sam died was to stop those feelings from ever developing. Max was my number one priority, as he always had been since his birth, but no longer did I think it was important to be earning a very healthy salary to provide for our traditional family unit. Now, there were much more important things than wealth. I'd never much cared for the spoils of cash anyway. Shiny new things are all well and good, but I'd rather put the money away for a rainy day. And these were our rainy days. It was the right thing to do, what I wanted to do, I didn't feel obliged, and I certainly didn't want my boy to ever think I'd made a personal sacrifice for his sake. The reality was he provided me with an infinitely more important and rewarding job – being his dad.

If anything, it's me that should be thanking him. As good as I am – on freakish occasions – I can't be at my best if he is too far away from me. Our situation is like the complete opposite of family units I'd seen examples of. Parents, particularly fathers, would say they simply couldn't think when their child was around, and that they needed peace and quiet to make sound decisions. With me, I craved Max, and always will do, at times when I really need to concentrate. He doesn't have to contribute to my thinking, just his presence brings me calm.

Of course, it would help if he shut up once in a while, too.

I've played field hockey for many years, off and on since I was a child, and in all that time I've probably scored less than ten goals. I took a break from the game during Samantha's pregnancy with Max and only returned when I decided I needed to get a little fitter again (one too many biscuits at one too many playgroups having taken their toll). I remember the first time Max came to watch. Some friends, and props, were arranged to keep him safe and occupied on the sidelines. I must have played a few hundred games of hockey, but this was the first in which I ever scored twice. Yes, not once, twice. Max wasn't looking on either occasion, but I'm convinced he was the reason.

I think that sums up my son's effect on me, and why I always want him around when I need to be at my very best. Because I can't be at my best without him.

I've of course tried to shelter him from the devastation of losing his mother, but at the same time I've not withheld the truth, or lied to make my life easier. When we've got an awkward question about where Max's mother was, I've always chosen to be open and upfront with those asking, and with Max listening.

I couldn't be sure how much he understood my explanations, and part of it was probably only preparation and practice for what was to come, but I taught my growing boy that his mother would always be part of him. She wasn't here, but he kept her in his heart, and he only needed to close his eyes to see her.

It was simultaneously heartbreaking and heart-warming to watch Max grow to understand what I was telling him, and for him to tell others the same when they asked him where his mother was. Being proud always, always, outweighed my sadness.

Children can be very accepting of any status quo, and say what's in their heads rather than reserve their judgement. And the younger they are, the more they seem to find the positive in things, or are able to change the subject from serious to silly in a heartbeat. One minute I'd be trying to explain heart failure to an inquisitive two-year-old. The next he'd lose interest in my answer and be more concerned about whether I had anything in my bag he could eat. Max taught me that while we mustn't ignore our past, life goes on.

And what a life it is at his side.

There is something very special between my son and I. I won't be the only parent to claim that, I know – I'd be in a minority if I didn't, even – but with Samantha's death, we've spent more time together, and experienced so much more as a duo, than we were ever set to. I've lost any parenting inhibitions I might have had in the process. There's nothing quite like a child encouraging you to dance around with a pink chiffon scarf at a playgroup full of women to blow things like that away. It has been the greatest privilege to have this time with my boy, and to be his dad.

It is difficult to say what we'd have been like had Sam not passed away, I don't really like to waste time thinking about it, and I also try to avoid painful grief triggers. If you find yourself in a scenario that has played out many times before with your now-deceased partner, it can be very difficult not to imagine them being there. People talk about ghosts, the scary type, but there isn't anything less scary than calling out to someone who's dead, by mistake or old habit. Waking up and momentarily forgetting that the person you shared your bed with for many years is not there. Sleepily reaching over, only to find space and sadness.

I can't say what it feels like to die. This book would be very short if I could. But I can say what it feels like to lose someone you loved. So many bereaved people express a wish to switch places with a lost one, that they'd give 'anything' to have one last moment with them, the chance to say something meaningful, poignant, the chance for one last kiss perhaps. But really, what would be the point? You'd be putting the person you loved through the most excruciating of pains, the thing that, if they really loved you, they feared the most – losing you.

I prefer to be grateful for my time with Samantha, and for the child our loving relationship created. She has always been, and remains, my constant inspiration to be a better person, and a better parent.

I've been asked many times what I want for my son as he grows, and I always default to the parenting cliché of choice. I want him to be happy.

But if I were being more selfish, and more honest, I would further that with the wish that he will continue to be the person he is today – compassionate, funny, intriguing, bright, positive, forceful, fun, mindful, considerate, selfish, lively, kind, caring, loving, loud and beautiful.

Basically, to always be my mini-colossus – just a few feet taller.

# Acknowledgements

There are many people without whom this book would not have come to fruition. I must first of all thank Samantha and Max for being my world and my inspiration always. Writing about my experiences with you has been both simultaneously painful and therapeutic. I truly hope that I have done justice to our story and the immense impact both of you had, and continue to have, on my life. You always have my love. Yours I carry with me too.

My sister also deserves massive recognition. I wasn't always nice to her – perhaps an understatement! – but I have always loved and respected her. She really stepped up when Samantha died, putting Max and I first in a lot of situations, without worrying about personal consequences. For that I'm truly grateful and will always be honoured to be her big brother, who is even more unbearable now that he has 'author' on his CV.

It was incredibly difficult for my parents to lose Samantha, too. They shielded me, as well as embraced me. Their generosity has uncomplicated my life. Once more I am grateful to them.

I thank Sam's family, always willing to care for their grandson, and who welcomed me into their lives and family. I hope they always think Sam made a good choice in me, and that they know Max will continue to be part of their lives, as Sam will in his.

I am blessed with some wonderful friends. The Foxs, The Wrights, The Hughes, The Subtlecliff-Stockton conglomerate, Lady B & her PMH Autoboobies, and many more I've neglected to mention. These are people who have been there with me at the right times, and made enormous contributions to my well-being, whether they knew it or not.

Those of the writing fraternity and Internet must also be thanked. Big hugs and kisses to Linda Aitchison who opened lots of doors for me, and to Lucy Jolin, who suggested I start writing a blog and encouraged me to continue. For the hundreds of fellow bloggers and readers who took note, and offered their support from all over the globe, thank you.

I'd like to thank the collective genius of New Holland Publishers who deemed it a good idea to commission me to write this book. I hope they still do.

And I reserve final praise for my wonderful Helen, for her love, understanding and support. Without her selfless encouragement to get this thing written – and help in finding the time around everything else to do it – it simply wouldn't be in your hands.